Running Free

SEBASTIAN COE
with David Miller

SIDGWICK & JACKSON
LONDON

First published in Great Britain in 1981 by Sidgwick and Jackson Limited

Copyright © 1981 Sebastian Coe and David Miller

The authors wish to thank the *Daily Express*, *The Guardian*, *The Sunday Telegraph*, *The Times*, *Athletics Weekly* and *Sports Illustrated* for permission to reproduce extracts and to draw upon original material. We also wish to express our gratitude to our families, for patience, support and enthusiasm given in many ways; likewise to close friends of Sebastian's. We just managed to meet the publishers' deadlines with unstinting assistance and advice from Marita Miller in the organization and typing of the text – of which Libby Joy was a sympathetic editor.

ISBN 0–283–98684–0

Typeset by Preface Ltd, Salisbury, Wilts.
and printed in Great Britain by
A. Wheaton & Co. Ltd, Exeter
for Sidgwick and Jackson Limited
1 Tavistock Chambers, Bloomsbury Way
London WC1A 2SG

For Peter . . . or was it
Percy?

Foreword

by Mary Peters, M.B.E.

(1972 Women's Pentathlon Gold Medallist and now British Women's Athletics Team Manager)

The first time I watched Sebastian Coe competing was at an indoor meeting at Cosford some years ago. I don't recall if he won, but I remember saying to his father Peter, 'Seb will be the pride of British Athletics in the future'. Little did I realize how soon Seb would be exciting huge crowds all over Europe.

Since Roger Bannister broke the four-minute mile in 1954, there have been many notable British middle distance runners – Ibbotson, Simpson, Whetton, Stewart, Foster. But none has caused the same excitement as Seb did in the 'Race of the Century': the 1,500 metres battle between Steve Ovett and Seb, with it's 'preview', the 800 metres. The world waited expectantly for their Moscow Olympic meetings.

I was on Village duty and sorry not to be able to see the 800 metres final live. Many of us considered Seb had the speed and style to win, but as Steve broke the tape those of us watching on television stood in stunned silence. Thrilled as we were by more gold and silver medals, we had felt the gold was meant for Seb.

I waited at the Village gate for his return, knowing his

disappointment. He blamed no one but himself, yet he proved his ability and character by fighting back to win the 1,500 metres. That took guts. I almost could not bear to watch the final, but it was a beautifully judged victory. Seb has met success and failure and remains unassuming. He will inspire youngsters for years to come to share the fitness, exhilaration and friendship which sport provides.

Contents

Illustrations

Introduction

Nice guys finish last, they say. This is the story of a young man who had the pulse of almost a whole sporting nation quickening for him because he personified so many of the aspirations of the anonymous. To millions, he was the quiet boy next door with the kind smile, a universally favourite son whose personal odyssey reached out and touched the soul of a nation down on its luck and drained of self-esteem. The fascination was as much whether a seemingly frail student might win a 1,500 metres foot race for Britain and raise the Union Jack in odious Russia, as the more fundamental human issue of whether virtue would triumph over largely self-inflicted adversity. If sport is a microcosm of life, then the events of the 1980 Olympic Games in Moscow were as turbulent as any medieval epoch. In reality, he was anything but the boy next door.

This is also, essentially, the story of a family, and of the father and son in particular: an ordinary English family who have managed not to take upon themselves false mantles because one of their four children became, in the space of a year, as well known a face on the television screen as the Prime Minister. It is the family ethic, too, which has helped endear him to the people at a time when the decline of the family, and of trust and respect between parents and children, is contributing to Western debility.

While Soviet and East German medals are heralded by their leaders as being symbolic of the supremacy of the mother state, it did not pass notice that in the gaining of many of Britain's medals there was an element of family achievement. Not only was there Sebastian Coe and his father Peter – his coach and constant companion, but Allan Wells and his altruistic wife Margot. There was also Sebastian's great rival Steve Ovett and his ever attentive mother Gay, while Daley Thompson acknowledged his debt to his Auntie Doreen, who had nurtured him since he was a child and was there in Moscow cheering. Gary Oakes, unexpected bronze medalist, owed much to his father, a north London coalman. Swimmer Sharon Davies was coached by her father, and Duncan Goodhew walked to the start wearing a cap belonging to the father who sadly did not live to see his son's triumph.

This book attempts to portray the quite remarkable relationship between an athlete and his father at the ultimate level of performance. Sebastian is singular because, in spite of his athletic excellence, he is adamant that this esoteric excellence should not dominate his life. His existence beyond the red ribbon of track in front of him is even more important than the medal at the finishing line: an attitude which, when coupled with an intense desire to be one of the greatest athletes in history, requires a very disciplined dedication. His medals and his records are the rewards of a brutal self-discipline largely unknown, or forgotten, in today's indulgent, insecure society.

I am aware that I run the risk of making Seb seem unrealistically a paragon, that I may stand accused of sycophantic prejudice; but the fact is that not only did heredity, the genetic accident of birth, grace him with unique physical and physiological attributes, but they are found in conjunction with an upbringing of love and application which has produced in him a serenity and an equanimity which I have observed in few world-famous sportsmen. He has adjusted to the burden of being taken for granted as public property with the patience of Job. Over recent years of mounting pressure and tension, I have waited for the moment when he might snap, but it has never come. While he has an absolute conviction in his spectacular ability, he is without conceit. Only once have I seen him even reproachful, and during the days of the most searching inner crisis an athlete can ever have had to endure, he unfalteringly exhibited a disarming outward calm. What the result of suppressing his feelings might have been had they not been gloriously released on the track we shall never know. He merely said: 'I never want to feel again what I felt after the 800 metres.'

The seed for this book was planted, I suppose, when I first went to interview an up and coming young athlete at Loughborough University shortly before his first international success in March 1977. A shy, dark-haired twenty-year-old came through the swing doors of the poshest pub in town, and over 'steak and two veg' and spotted-dog pudding, modestly explained how he was aiming to 'peak' for the Moscow Olympics on the absurdly low training mileage of thirty-five miles a week.

He thought he might one day specialize in the 5,000 metres, in which an 800 metres potential 'of hopefully 1 minute 45 seconds' would be useful. Little did either of us know – though perhaps, on second thoughts, he had an inkling – that in just over two years he would shatter that 1:45 'potential' and, with it, the 800 metres world record. What was apparent then was his crisp, clear view of his objectives, and a rational assessment of his own particular qualities which somehow made you sit forward on the edge of your chair and forget you had a train back to London to catch. When, a few days later, running blisteringly from the front, he won the European Indoor 800 metres with a time a fraction outside the world indoor record, I wrote in the *Daily Express*:

'The boy – for physically that is almost what he still is at twenty – who ran away with the European Indoor title in San Sebastian is about to pick up the torch where Brendan Foster put it down after Montreal. The stage is ready for a duel which will give athletics the kind of spectacle it has not had since the days of Bannister, Chataway, Pirie, and Ibbotson – between the quiet-spoken Coe and confident, extrovert Steve Ovett. Both these gifted but vastly different young runners are capable of getting close to, if not beating, world record times for 800 or 1,500 metres. Coe reckons he may ultimately move up to 5,000 metres. Yet they are still three years or so off their peak, which will optimistically coincide with the Moscow Olympics. Their personal rivalry, as yet unfurled, should be as great a spur as any medal. Ovett, so disappointing in Montreal when he misjudged his tactics in the outside lane of the 800 metres final, has spent the winter ploughing through the mud of cross-country runs. Coe, inwardly confident but as modest as Ovett tends to be brash, has been working at basic speed with spectacular results. There is no question that Ovett has one of the most superb physiques of any middle distance runner in the world, with untold strength. But Coe has shown, by going to the front in San Sebastian after 200 metres and staying there, that his relatively light body conceals enormous reservoirs of power. It is sad that almost by definition Olympic champions must be odd-birds and loners. Coe at the moment appears to be madly normal. We shall wait and see what a summer in the limelight will do to him, but I fancy he is heat resistant.'

What now began to catch the public's eye was a runner who was like no runner they had seen before. While Ovett, who had matured earlier, exuded power in the manner of Montreal Olympic champion John Walker of New Zealand, Coe's running gave an ethereal sensation that he was floating. He was in the race but somehow apart from it, and every time he ran there was an aura of destiny. 'Effortless power' is a cliché of my trade but if ever an athlete possessed it, here it was. When I was eighteen, and a modest junior sprinter, I had competed in the August Bank Holiday British Games at the White City, and had been overawed to be warming up on the centre of the track at the same time as an athlete whom I revered, the twice Olympic 800 metres champion Mal Whitfield of the United States. For twenty-four years I regarded Whit-

field as the supreme stylist, a beautifully relaxed runner
who changed pace so imperceptibly that spectators and
rivals alike could measure the change only by the gap
which opened. Now, here was the flowing gracefulness in
a British runner. Moreover, the set of his head upon his
shoulders and the cadence of his limbs imparted an
aesthetic quality which further aroused the public's
acclaim. In the moment of his triumph in Moscow the
New Statesman would refer to him – without exaggeration
– as the Nureyev of the track. It was that cadence for
which Peter Coe had been striving throughout the twelve
years and thousands of hours of training. The father's
achievement in navigating his son from fourteen-year-old
wraith to Olympic champion and world record breaker is
a coaching phenomenon probably without parallel in the
history of sport.

Part of the understanding I struck up with Seb, even
though he is young enough to be my son, stemmed from
the fact of our mutual experiences, sometimes amusing, of
having enthusiastic, mildly eccentric fathers from a patri-
archal, almost Victorian-London background. In spite of
having little initial knowledge of the sport, but proffering
substantial encouragement, my father was largely instru-
mental in my reaching the fringe of the 1956 Olympic
soccer team, and I became intrigued by the inter-action
between Seb and his father even when the son had
reached such a peak of proficiency: a synthesis of mutual
pride and ambition.

When he was fifteen and was asked by Angela, his
mother, what would happen if he did not achieve what he
wanted in athletics, Seb had replied simply that he would
find a sport at which he *could* succeed. Privately he had
been motivated by the example of Jonah Barrington who,
when a near alcoholic at Trinity College, Dublin, had
determined to make himself into world squash champion
within two years, even though he could hardly play the
game. The difference for Seb, of course, was that he was
already highly proficient at something.

Early in 1979 I had discussions with Sigdwick and Jackson about the possibility of writing a book on the Moscow

Olympics, and when it was discovered that they had had
the idea of a book about Sebastian Coe it was natural that
the two should be merged. Since then Seb has also
achieved the sensational coup of three world records in
forty-one days. This book is neither a biography nor an
autobiography – for, as Seb would insist, his life still lies
ahead – but is an account of one athlete's quest for
success.

The success has not only earned him fame, about which
he remains equivocal, but affection on an unpre-
cedented scale, from young and old alike, and from many
who would normally take scant interest in sport. It is
probable that he is our most popular sportsman since
Henry Cooper and Bobby Charlton were in their prime. He
was voted sportsman of the year by wide margins by the
Sports Writers' Association of Great Britain and in the
Daily Express poll, taken from its readers, in both 1979
and 1980. After winning the 1,500 metres in Moscow he
received more than 4,000 telegrams, letters, and cards of
congratulation and good wishes, many of them sent
anonymously by humble people not seeking, however dis-
tantly, to associate themselves with the achievement but to
express appreciation of it: 'Three Brits in Paris', 'Two
admirers in Bristol', 'All the girls on the telephone
exchange at Harlow'; and so on, endlessly. From school
children to retired nurses living alone with their cats came
the common message of shared happiness. Over two
months after the race, 10 October was the first day on
which the post brought nothing. Of course it is unhealthy
for people to sublimate their lives too far to the sporting
exploits of others, as happens in our great football cities.
But in 1979 and 1980 Sebastian Coe gave to others an
elixir, that hope of better things which famous deeds give
us to draw upon freely.

Not that he was aware of all this in Moscow, where he
was conscious only of his daunting test of nerve and
character. It was later that he admitted: 'It never sank in
at the time what it would mean if I lost the 1,500 metres.
Not even in the darkest moments after the 800 metres did
it concern me how it might affect others. It was a week or

so later, suddenly, when I was out training at home, that I broke into a cold sweat with the realization of what I had been carrying in terms of public goodwill, of the years of effort put in by family and friends, and it was a little frightening.'

Ironically, the same factor which placed tremendous pressure upon him simultaneously gave him the nerve to survive that pressure: the belief, shared with only a few and still doubted by some, that he had the ability, the sheer unrivalled class, to win both races in Moscow whatever way they were run. I believed it then and now, yet, because of his defeat in the 800 metres, the ultimate proof of his supremacy is still to come. It will come, I am sure. Such was his confidence that he had even said before the Games, in answer to those who questioned his stamina, that he would like the heats, the semi-finals and the final of the 1,500 metres to be run all on the same day, 'and then let's see what happens'.

We know what *did* happen.

January, 1981   DAVID MILLER

Publisher's Note

To differentiate between the authors, text by
Sebastian Coe appears within bold quotation marks

1: Beginnings

‘Some of my earliest recollections are of running. Looking back it seems that from the time I could walk I preferred to run. It just seemed natural. When I was still quite young we moved from London to Stratford-on-Avon because of my father's work. We lived on the edge of the town and I would regularly run two miles or so into town and back again on errands for my mother, never using a bicycle, preferring the feeling of running. I can remember jogging beside my sister Miranda's pram, which must have been when I was no more than three. When we went for picnics in the Cotswolds, I would open and close the gates and then run behind the car. I never walked anywhere, it seems. I had a genuine, instinctive love of running, so that even between the ages of twelve and seventeen, when the rewards of training were not always immediate or tangible, self-motivation was never a problem. In becoming my coach my father made sacrifices, of course, though he never really voiced them. It is impossible to know by how much he might have advanced his engineering career had he not devoted the time he has to my coaching. Yet I have made my own sacrifices, as every runner does – training in the morning, then the gym at lunchtime, training again in the late afternoon, all fitted around the business of keeping an academic programme up to scratch. The evening comes and you'd like to go out,

but you are just too tired. As Brendan Foster has said,
'running is just feeling tired all the time'. There are days
when walking round a department store, or even walking
up stairs, can almost kill you. When I spent the winter
before the Olympics living and training outside Rome,
staying with friends, the public, had they known where I
was, would have had visions of *la dolce vita*. How wrong
they would have been! The reality was falling asleep in a
chair in the evening, knowing that Rome, with all it had to
offer, was twenty minutes down the road, while I was
slumped there, often alone – me and the BBC world service!**'**

———

Sebastian Newbold Coe was born in Chiswick, West London on 29 September, 1956, the autumn during which the
celebrated Russian ballerina Ulanova was enrapturing
audiences at Covent Garden, and Peter Coe had returned
to England from business in America specially so that
his first child should be born at home. The threads of
heredity and environment which would ultimately, on a
sunny afternoon in Moscow, lead to the most coveted
honour an athlete can win, were coloured as much by artis-
tic inheritance and influence as robust physical endow-
ments.

His mother, Angela, had been an enthusiastic repertory
actress before her marriage. Angela's own connection with
ballet and theatre would inevitably have some physical
significance for the children – her own mother had danced
with the legendary Pavlova, and Seb's sister would become
a ballet dancer. If you could not write, paint, or dance in
her family you were unusual. When Angela married Peter
Coe, who had diligently and extensively qualified himself as
a production engineer, there was some surprise among the
family: engineering to many people still had overtones of oil
rather than the drawing-board. The designing of industrial
machinery was one of those areas unknown to vast numbers
of the British middle-class, whose educational prejudice in
favour of the arts has so shaped and limited Britain's

industrial status in the second half of the twentieth century. (As for running, that was something one occasionally did to keep healthy.)

━━━━━━━

‘My mother's mother, who is half Irish and half Welsh, was the daughter of an artist who was an R.A., and she herself had to give up dancing when she broke an ankle. On my father's side, his grandfather, Robert Coe, was a sprinter from Sunderland in his youth, competing against the north-east professionals, 'so fast he could kick over a rabbit' they used to say. But his son Percy, my grandfather, was never a sportsman, suffering for a long time from a bad leg. He was a small business-man, a carpenter-shopfitter, who worked a lot in Regent Street, and lived until he was seventy-three. My father's mother was the daughter of Harry Newbold, something of an eccentric, who was born with a silver spoon in his mouth and was sent to boarding school in Scotland when his parents died young. He was an engineer who was also involved in the circus and the vaudeville stage. He knew Chaplin, and was still roller-skating when he was eighty-two. Before she married Percy Coe my grandmother had often had to stay with her grandparents in Walkley, then a village on the moors just outside Sheffield, when her parents were on tour. Today, ironically, Walkley is only half a mile from our house within the city itself.’

━━━━━━━

Violet, Peter's mother, is the personification of the London which endured the Blitz, of the Flanagan and Allen line, 'Who do you think you are, Mr Hitler?' If Seb's equanimity comes from his mother, and in turn, quite probably, from her father, it is easy to see where the Churchillian resolve which lifted his spirit in Moscow came from. Granny Violet has that kind but firm demeanour which would have seen Rommel off with an umbrella. At an international at Crystal Palace, she was the only person in the grandstand to remain seated during the German national anthem. Her son is also slightly formidable. Peter, a tall, slim man who was a more than competent club racing cyclist in his younger days, is unquestionably an authoritarian. When peering over or through his dark-rimmed glasses he bears more than a passing resemblance to the cartoonist Giles's schoolmaster, Old Chalky. Yet behind the austere exterior beats a sensitive heart. Unerringly, he knew his own son, who – like many small boys – had something of the appearance of a young giraffe in the early days. He would need the most careful, sensitive coaching.

'He was a very nervous young boy, he suffered from nervous eczema as well as pollen asthma. He was incredibly sensitive. He was deeply shocked when he failed his 11-plus, but as always I gave it to him straight, saying, "you can either be a Secondary Mod drop-out, or get down to it and get your 'O' levels". He grafted and grafted, and got eight 'O' levels. He was, I think, the only one of the four children who would let me stand behind him and shove. He always had an ability to get the maximum out of what he's got.'

The outsider might wonder whether Peter was disposed to propel Seb more than he might have done for the very reason that his pushing was accepted. He was, one senses, disappointed when slim, feline Miranda, who was with the Royal Ballet and then the Ballet Rambert, ultimately gave up ballet to become a cabaret dancer in Las Vegas, subsequently switching to modelling in New York, and then back to cabaret in Paris. Nicholas, the family wit and court-jester, had the makings of an outstanding competitive cyclist, until he suffered a cycling accident while doing a paper round and thereafter never put his undoubtedly fine physique to the test again. Emma, the youngest – now post-'O' levels, forever laughing infectiously, often at herself – gives you the impression she would love to be pushed but is not quite sure where to. Binding the house together is Angela, self-effacing, patient counsellor to all five others, the soft pedal subtly shaping her husband's cadenza.

Theirs is a happy, solid, busy, rambling household up on a hill beside Sheffield University, the rear view overlooking a large university recreation area directly below the garden, where Seb has done much of his laborious repetitive sprint training. The city lies a few minutes down the hill and in the other direction, equally close, is the vastness of the Derbyshire Peak District, spreading across the Pennines. There, runner and coach have painstakingly welded their remarkable, enduring partnership. Peter says:

'Until a few years ago I drove both of us hard, patience was not my virtue. I expected him to be ready on the dot for training! But he was a splendid fellow, he knew better how to live with me than anyone in the family. He learned obedience, yet by the time he grew up his father wasn't God, he knew that I had feet of clay. We worked on a programme and he never badgered me or questioned the programme. At fourteen I knew he was good, at sixteen I felt a strange kind of certainty that if I was patient I had a world beater. At that time we could not be sure of the distance and would probably have said 5,000 metres, but already he was veering towards the 1,500 metres.'

❦I remember arriving at Tapton School in Sheffield halfway through an academic year, also the strangeness of being in a big city for the first time, and playing nothing but soccer. In my first game I played madly for an hour, rushing all over the place trying to tackle everyone to prove myself with the bigger boys. The master in charge was John O'Keefe, I thought he was terrific and I wanted to be able to play like him. He was a bit like the master in the film *Kes*, only John didn't show off like him. John was very good to me and it was with him that I stayed out in Rome – he moved there to an English school some time ago. Failing the 11-plus was one of the best

things that happened to me. Going to Tapton, a big-city
school, I found a large social mix; it was a very good
school within the state system, a sort of 'people's Eton'.
It was tough, and more character-building than a small
grammar school would have been. Some of those I knew
when we lived in Stratford who went to the grammar
school have done less well academically than many of
those at Tapton. We were a form of 'failed 11-plus', yet
many have come through and had university educations,
getting degrees. Of my five best friends, all emphatic fail-
ures at eleven, one got a first in physics at Sheffield,
another a first in maths at Warwick, and two got degrees
in English at Liverpool. We came through as fighters.

Peter always has an unbending attitude to my academic
side as well as to my running, and if athletics hadn't been
able to become an academic thing with him, almost intellectual, he wouldn't have been so interested. He was never
one for the gossip and the old wives' tales of the sport, and
I suppose that attitude has rubbed off on me. I would be
very surprised, as far as he is concerned, if his attitude
didn't contain an element of wanting to produce something just for the hell of it – in a totally natural way –
pushing potential into new areas. When people have said
to him in the past, 'You've let it become an intellectual
exercise', his answer was, 'you're dead right!' I couldn't
have asked more from him. Being an engineer he was
good at maths, but didn't know much about statistics. In
order to be able to help me with my Statistics 'A' level he
enrolled two nights a week as a mature student at a local
college. I can't think that I would do that for any of my
kids. But if that seems too serious, taking things too far,
he retained a balance. When I was fifteen, we went over
to Stretford for a league race, and when we got back
home late there was no time left for revision for a CSE
paper the next day. (I had to do both CSE and 'O' level.)
I said, 'that's the end of my CSE!' but Peter merely said,
'you're better off with the 1:56 for the 800 metres which
you got this afternoon'. In the event I got both.

He was always particularly good when it came to
injuries, insisting we treat them with the utmost respect,

and that I should never run through them as some people
do. When we were out on runs on the moors when I was
young, he would take me down the long, steep inclines by
car, so that I should not damage the bones while they
were still growing, and then make me work uphill where
the stress is only on the muscles. It is when things go
wrong that a good coach is priceless. I always remember
what David Hemery said at a coaching course for schoolboys: 'You're all going to get injuries and the true worth
of an athlete will always come to the fore when he is
injured.' Two weeks later I found I had stress fractures of
the shins in spite of Peter's caution, and was out of competition for a year – a very trying year. **,**

It would be difficult to over-estimate the contribution
made by Angela to Seb's ascent of Olympian heights. She
has been strong without being too demonstrative, supporting without being fussy, influential without interfering,
bringing to the intensity of a situation the soothing minis-
trations of a mother and a wife. Throughout the arduous
years in which the man and the boy were continually driving towards a distant and not always clearly defined objective, she was able to hold the emotional tiller as they
negotiated rapids which at various times could have cap-
sized one or both of them.

'I suppose I first realized how serious Seb was when we
came to Sheffield and, at the age of twelve, he joined
Hallamshire Harriers. For a long time I thought Peter
was going barmy over someone who wasn't going to be
exceptional. I was amazed that Seb never complained at
the routine, at the sheer pain in his hands from the cold
when he came back from training sometimes in mid-
winter up on the hills, when he was told how many
hours' sleep he had to have! He had a wide circle of
friends, yet he willingly opted out of social events. At
his 'O' level stage I felt it was very much in the balance
whether he continued. Even Christmas Day had a

timetable, including training and, say, two hours' geography revision. I can remember Peter saying, "you can do it, one helps the other". Seb managed it all, and the same with 'A' levels, his self-discipline was astonishing. There were times in the early days when I wished, I suppose, that he wasn't so good at running. Sports days were embarrassing and I'd find myself thinking, "*please lose something*". You could hear other mothers muttering, "it's only going to be Coe again, I don't know why we bother to come". For years I accepted Peter's saying, "he's going to be world class" while I was tending to think to myself, "I just hope it doesn't blow up in his face". I didn't want either of them to be disappointed. Because I saw less of what was happening up there on the hills, I suppose I probably had less faith in the ultimate sucesss.'

———

‘In some respects you could say my mother has been even more important in helping towards what I've done than Peter; not down on the track or working out my training schedules, but in providing a solid base for everyone in the house, in maintaining an air of consistency and continuity. For every extra training session, for every extra race, it means a whole day reorganized in terms of meals and laundry and so on. My mother is very level-headed, very easy going, and has a sense of humour, which as far as I am concerned is more important than anything. She has cushioned us against a lot of the anxieties, although athletics itself is marvellous for releasing pent up feelings. People say never play cards with a really successful sportsman because they have to win whatever they are doing. But these days I can never be bothered to be aggressive about anything *outside* athletics, and my aggression on the track is all inside. It was different when I was younger. Miranda and Nick say that when I was eight or nine I used to throw down the bat if I was out when I was playing cricket, or claim it was the wind which had taken off the bails. I was very nervous for at least three days before a race in school events. But learning to control athletic nerves helped control exam nerves eventually. I threw away the 11-plus, but now I can sleep without problem the night before a big race or examinations. **’**

One of his early reports at Tapton, for French lessons, records that 'his manner in class tends to arrogance', but by the time he was fourteen one of his masters would write: 'I feel I must comment on the very real help Sebastian gives to Danny.' By one of those strange twists of coincidence, the future Olympic champion had become friendly with Danny Heffernan, a boy afflicted with a burden of physical misfortune beyond the imagination of any normally fit person. Suffering when young from a rare form of juvenile arthritis, Danny received treatment which is at this time still a matter of arduous litigation. Whether or not the drugs treatment was responsible, Danny lost all but the quarter sight of one eye and his growth was retarded to the extent that, although the same age as Seb, he still has the build of an eleven-year-old. He has had countless operations, including on both hips, yet in spite of all this, in spite of coordinating his own legal battle when able to read only Braille – though legal charities have recently stepped in – he has retained one of the warmest and happiest dispositions you could meet, thanks in no small part to the friendship of Seb and his family. There were times, during periods of intense pain, when he was nursed as if one of the family by Angela and Peter.

‘ Danny and I had some rare old times at school. We had a nice little line going in orange drinks on sports day, only a penny or two, until we were rumbled, and there were other extra-mural trading deals in government surplus compasses and remaindered annuals! Danny was a marvellous character, he was so independent in spite of his handicap. It used to take a lot of self-control on my part

when we were walking down the hill after school. He
would insist on carrying his own briefcase and all the
other boys would be belting past us while we had to go
along at Danny's very slow pace. The way he has fought
against his disability, living alone in his own purpose-built
flat, and the way he has retained his sense of humour, are a
lesson for us all. **>**

Seb's prowess was now such that one indulgent master
would occasionally allow him to slip away from religious
instruction periods to put in some extra training. In the
winter of 1970–1, never out of the first three, he won the
Yorkshire Schools cross-country title, and was building up
towards the English Schools meeting at Luton. A week or
so beforehand, Peter sent him out one afternoon for an
easy distance run on the steep gradients of the surrounding streets. He got slightly carried away.

< Maybe it was coming first in the Yorkshire,
maybe it was just natural enthusiasm, but I started racing
a bus up one of the longer hills, ignoring Peter's instructions to take it easy. He was away on business and not
there to pace me in the car as usual. I kept catching the
bus up between stops and really having a bit of fun. It was
sheer bravado. I came back home and said to Peter at
supper time, 'you should have seen the bus driver's face!'
Peter gradually became more and more angry, and I was
so stiff I couldn't train for two days. I never again disre-
garded his training instructions and readily agreed, 'you
make the decisions, I'll do the running'. In recognition, I
suppose, of my prospects at Luton, the school sent down
two bus-loads of supporters. I ran like a drain and came
twenty-fourth. I felt awful, but the other boys had had
a nice day out, and I was allowed off homework for a
couple of nights. **>**

Whatever that failure, any idea of becoming a professional footballer, thoughts of a trial with Sheffield Wednesday, were now in the past, and as for rugby, there was not much prospect for a half-pint of six and a half stone. His course was irrevocably settled, even though that summer, for the first and only time in his life, he came last in a 1,500 metres in the English Schools Championships.

―――――――

〈 I'd had a mouth operation for some teeth trouble and had been out of action for five weeks, missing all my exams. I'd been staying down in Sidcup overnight before the race with friends who had a flat over a greengrocer's shop, with the result that I was awake at five in the morning. It was this experience, among others, which led Peter to devise a pre-race formula which I have been working to ever since, wherever circumstances permit. As Peter said, it was vital to produce myself friction-free for the race, physically and mentally fresh. The worst thing about schoolboys, and even some adults, is that they tend to run the race ten times beforehand and that's why it's so much better to keep out of the way. It does of course mean it's vital to know the race schedule and to be sure that it won't be altered. I was not popular with schoolmasters when Peter started insisting I should travel on the day of the race and not with the team, but there is no doubt about the psychological value of being away from a group. It led to some snide jokes around the northern circuit, that I would only arrive half an hour before the start in a plain black van, but I didn't mind that. By now I knew where I wanted to go, and I could put up with the difficulties which arose from being 'different'. On one occasion Angela remembers my saying that if I couldn't be successful at athletics I would find a sport where I could be. There were quite a few friends present in the house – Ian Hague, for instance, a good 400 metres man who represents the essence of the sport, a purist who, while being my friend, has always been emphatic about what a great athlete Steve Ovett is, and others involved in the sport like

Robert Hague and John Henson. My statement didn't
offend them: there was just a stunned silence and it was
clear to me I was simply operating on a different concept.
George Gandy, who became my coach at Loughborough,
has always said that quite apart from the physiological
aspects required to be a champion there has to be an
insatiable *need* to succeed. **'**

===============

The next two years saw a steady improvement in Seb's
progress with the inevitable fluctuations which occur
among boys growing at different rates in their teens. In
1972 he came tenth in the English Schools intermediate
cross-country over four miles at Hillingdon, running
against boys a year older – including Ovett who, at that
time a 400 metres runner on the track, finished second. The following year, now sixteen, was a good one for
him: he won the Yorkshire Schools 3,000 metres in very
bad conditions at York in 8:49, then the English Schools
3,000 metres at Bebington in 8:40·2. To these victories
were added the Northern Counties 1,500 metres in 3:59·5
– his first in under four minutes – and the Amateur Athletics Association Youth Championships 1,500 metres in
3:55. It was this result at Aldersley on 4 August, 1973,
which more than any so far convinced Peter that Seb
could go all the way.

===============

'The next year was miserable. In the spring of
1974 I went on a national coaching week at Lilleshall,
instead of a geography field week in Swanage, as a result
of which I was decidedly unpopular with masters at
Abbeydale Grange School, where I had moved after taking 'O' levels at Tapton. I was even less popular when,
asked in class what Bakersfield, California was famous for
– the largest refinery in the world – I replied instead, 'it's
where Jim Ryun broke the world record 1,500 metres in
1963 with 3:51·2'. It wasn't long after that I found that I

had two stress fractures and was unable even to train from the end of April to September. But I had a good winter, and early next year at Cleckheaton went under 3:50 for 1,500 metres for the first time with 3:49·7. Soon after this I had a minor injury, and as we never took risks I went two weeks with no training. I hadn't really thought about the Yorkshire Senior Championships at the end of May, but after a few satisfactory 800 metres workouts Peter suddenly announced, in that dramatic way he rather fancies, 'we're going to run'. Aged eighteen, I was nervous and anxious about my first senior race. We went out to a jazz club that night and I stayed until after eleven, thinking to myself, 'has he flipped, or have I?' The following day I won, slowing up, against Walter Wilkinson, a hard, gritty Yorkshire train driver. If the British Athletics Board put up a Mercedes as an incentive, Walter would still get into the Olympic team today. He really was a competitor.

A personal best of 8:14·2 for 3,000 metres in the Northern Counties Under Twenty Championships at Blackburn ranked me junior number two in Europe, and I followed this with a personal best 3:47·1 to win the AAA Junior 1,500 metres. Now came my first experience of the strange lack of official cooperation which existed for so long at international level. I won the AAA with bad blisters, and asked if I could be excused the Junior International against France and Spain so as to get fit for the European Junior Championships in Athens. But I was obliged to run in the International.

Athens was a great experience for me. Dear Jim Coote, Athletics Correspondent of the *Daily Telegraph*, who was so committed and was always there even at many of the lesser meetings, had criticized my selection for Athens, saying I was selected on my record rather than my potential. I took no offence because he so obviously cared a lot about the sport, and it was a tragedy for all of us when he crashed piloting his own light aircraft down to Turin in 1979 for the Europa Cup Final. I loved the heat in Athens and I was really relaxed before the race – so relaxed that I fell asleep on a couch in an empty dressing-room under the stadium an hour before the final, and only

woke up eighteen minutes before the start. Although I ran
a new personal best of 3:45·2, I was third behind Ari
Paunonen of Finland. I remember afterwards receiving a
lecture from Mrs Nelson Neale, a nice old lady who, I was
told, was a Women's AAA coach even though she seemed
well into her seventies. She told me very earnestly how
Sydney Wooderson's failing in pre-war days had been that
he couldn't change pace and that this was why I had lost. I
thanked her, but I couldn't help smiling.

The one thing that really did irritate me, an indication
of the kind of immaturity and irresponsibility which often
exists in British teams travelling abroad, was that while I
was asleep one night in the student village somebody took
all my racing kit, and pinned a ransom note on the wall
saying it would turn up again 'in Moscow 1980'! I don't
think it affected my equilibrium, it just seemed silly. On
the way back, coming through customs at London, people
put a lot of excess duty-free stuff on my trolley, voting me
the one with the most innocent face. I was the only one
who got stopped!**

Every mother's gold medal—
Angela with her first baby
(3 months)

'On your marks' (5 months)

'That Russian over there
looks a bit good' (18 months)

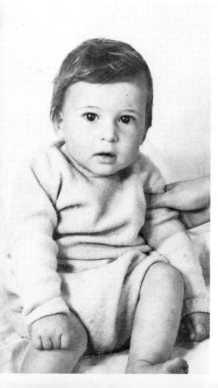

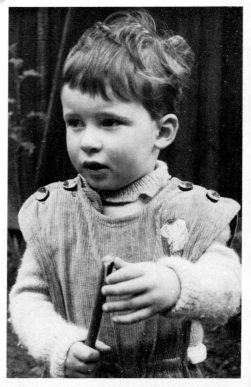

'I'd like the bloke even if he wasn't my father.' With Peter in Pembrokeshire (4 years)

'Do I really want all this hassle?' (3 years)

'I think this girl could be fun!' With Miranda (6 and 4 years)

'Why does this joker have to pick on me?' With Nick (10 and 5 years)

'I'm sure it clipped the line.'
Leamington (10 years)

All good friends.
Miranda (9), Nick (5), and Seb (11)

'The loneliness, the solitude, the
remoteness . . . so stimulating.'
On Mam Tor (12 years)

Winning a club relay at Rotherham in
1970 (13 years)

First sports day at Tapton School:
hurdles concentration (second from
right, 12 years)

'And in lane one we have an exciting newcomer!' Emma (3) on right, Nick (5), Miranda (9), and Seb (11)

First home, Sheffield Schools 1,500m
(14 years)

Leading round the last bend,
English Schools 3,000m at Bebington
(16 years)

Family holiday in
St Malo (17 years)

Sheffield City Schools Cross Country at Graves Park. Aged 13—and only a year younger than Hallam Harriers colleague Neil Hopkins (behind)

(*Sheffield Newspapers Ltd*)

Coach and athlete beside the track, the partnership of the past twelve years
(Bela Domokos)

(Daily Mail)

(Bela Domokos)

**(Below) Miranda showing her paces on a New York sidewalk during a break from modelling
(Left) The same poise as her brother has on the track**
(Daily Mail)

(Bela Domoko

Seb and Peter discuss tactics at Crystal Palace before a Loughborough-Southern Counties match. A scene repeated a hundred times

2: Life with Father

‘The partnership with my father has worked because I like the guy. I would like him even if he were not my father. He can be a bit brutal, certainly, but he has been right so often. When I was only thirteen he drew up a projection of progress for me to 1980 with an optimum 1,500 metres time of 3:30, and that at a time when I had achieved only 4:31·8 and the world record was still Herb Elliott's 3:35·6 in the Rome Olympic final. So often over the years he's had more faith in me than I have had in myself. I know I can rely on him one hundred per cent. Anyone who levels the accusation that he was on an ego trip, that he was force-feeding me, is way off the mark. I never complained because I shared with him the hope and ambition that he always had for me. There's no county in England to rival Yorkshire for the mile talent which has come out of it, with men like Ibbotson and Simpson, but initially a lot of people thought my old man was right off his head. 'He's killing him', they would say, and Peter's reply would merely be, 'that's right, all the way to the top'. His greatest achievement, I think, was in getting me over the difficult transitional period from junior to senior ranks four or five years ago. When I was seventeen he said to me that if ever I felt I was not going far enough or fast enough with him, that I needed a different coach, I should say so. But the moment passed, and I never doubted him.

There was no recrimination from either side over poor results. We were both free agents. If anything ever struck me as crazy, I'd say so beforehand. Even after Prague in 1978, when we agreed I should run from the front and got well beaten into third place, there were no problems. Some critics thought we were both mad, but it was no lie when Peter said, 'I learnt more from that one race than anything in the whole year'. What is special about him as a coach is that he thinks on his feet, as they say in the north. He is one of nature's survivors. There's nothing I do that isn't thought out, not a single action is casual. But he's not a motivator – that's not necessary in either training or racing because I'm a self-motivator. Funnily enough, one of the most important features of our relationship, possibly the key, is that he knew nothing about coaching when he started! The fact that he didn't compete left him without mental barriers on what is physically possible.

If he'd competed, even at a lesser level, he would have had an idea what 10 × 400 metres in 60 seconds actually *feels* like, and he would have been conditioned by that. On the physiological side he's read very widely. His talent is as much in *management* as in coaching. In the early days he would go out and find the right advice on technicalities. Now he doesn't need much advice. There was a time when he was continually going to coaching and physiology conferences, constantly picking people's brains. That is where George Gandy has been so valuable to us, with his specialist knowledge in bio-mechanics.*

———

George Gandy, a tall, dark, sardonic humourist, athletics consultant to Sudan and the Irish Army, is a man whose rolling glances, from behind heavy rimmed glasses, occasionally give him the air of a Balkan spy in a Bond thriller. Such an air befits someone who possesses a Greek-like capacity for getting his own way without anyone noticing. He is not only an authority on bio-mechanics, but is an athletics coach of considerable per-

ception who has been responsible for much of Loughborough University's prominence in recent years. His contribution to Seb's progress, the humour apart, has been a
vital one with winter speed work, circuit training, and
weight training, in the thirty weeks of the academic year
when Seb has unavoidably been separated from Peter.
In the winter prior to his three world records in 1979,
Seb, maintaining a full academic life at Loughborough,
trained no more than around fifty miles a week, which by
international standards of the day was strangely low when
the school of thought since 1960 was that mileage made
champions. Led by the coaching example of New Zealander Arthur Lydiard, who trained Peter Snell and others, at
least one hundred miles a week had become the norm,
and indeed there were those who trained far in excess of
this, with the result that many of them ultimately and
inevitably broke down with muscle and joint injuries. It
was Peter Coe who reminded everyone that quantity was
no substitute for quality.

———————

‘ Round about the end of my junior career we
really decided there had to be a change of emphasis. I was
being labelled a 1,500 metres or 3,000 metres runner at
eighteen. By twenty-one I'd probably have been running
5,000 metres; before I was thirty I would have been running marathons. That was not what I wanted. I wanted to
run 1,500 metres. There's only a limited possibility of
improvement in distance work, going up and up and up,
but coming back down again we could see the benefits
were very much better. I needed the leg speed. My stride
length had never been a problem, but on occasion maintaining a fast cadence was. I wasn't going to be able to
develop my cadence or my sprinting abilities just from
running distances or going up the clock all the time. I had
to be getting in with the sprinters, I had to find out what
it was actually like to sprint. That was really the side of
my Loughborough career, when I started training with
George in the winter months, developing leg speed with

weight training and speed drills. My advice, if anybody
wants it, is not to get too far away from the basis of what
you are doing, because modern 800 metres and 1,500
metres running demands a considerable amount of leg
speed and you're not going to get it from running slowly
in training. You have to develop and train the mind, as
well as the body, to run fast. A lot of it is coordination.
You cannot improve your basic speed, unfortunately.
It's a fact that we are born with what we are born with.
You can't alter your muscle composition. The important
thing is to work on strengths and not on weaknesses.
Sometimes in the winter of 1978 and 1979 my mileage
was considerably less than fifty a week. Obviously I don't
need so many miles because of my light build, and I am
not willing to smash my feet and knees out on the road. I
am lucky that I've never needed to cram in the distance
work. 9

Was not the double relationship with Peter, as athlete and
son, inhibiting?

&No, it's the proof of the success of our coach/ath-
lete relationship that I didn't feel the need to escape from
him in the home, that we could coexist happily across the
dinner table. But I have never allowed him to organize
my life outside athletics. His attitude on matters away from
athletics is, 'that's my advice on my experience, it's up to
you what you do with it'. From his own family, he has
brought a great unity to us as a family and we always show
a united public front. He's been criticized for talking about
'my athlete', rather than 'my son', or telling people 'we're
going to run in Oslo'. But I would say in just the same way
'we're going to run a 1,500', it's something we're in
together. Certainly, he's a hard man. I know from the men
down at the cutlery factory where he's production director,
and where I've worked in the holidays. They've told me:

'He's tough but fair. He's consistent, you always know
where you stand with him.'

Once, when we were having dinner, there was a call
from the works manager. 'The bloody factory's on fire'
Peter said, as he dashed out of the front door and down
the hill in the car through all the red lights. It was all a bit
of a farce, the fire-brigade couldn't find it and rang up in
the middle of the fire to ask for the post code! The block
was shared with another business which the company had
attempted to buy out several times. It was this, in fact, which
was now on fire, and not Peter's own factory. 'It looks like
it's yours overnight', said the dejected owner as he stood
beside Peter, surveying the smoking, gutted building. 'I
was going to pull it down anyway', Peter said rather crushingly!

People who infer, from his public reaction to the mess I
made of the 800 metres in Moscow, that he dominates me
would not have thought the same had they been there at
the open-air café in the Olympic Village when I learned
what he had said to the press the day after the race. I told
him quite emphatically, 'you're supposed to be an articulate man, but your choice of words was naïve. I'll accept
the criticism from you direct, but I won't take it from you
via the press.' Peter can be too trusting in assuming the
best in people who have power like the press. You can be
friendly with the media on a personal basis, but in the
final analysis they have a job to do, and that will always
be their priority ahead of personal allegiance. So you have
to be guarded in moments of stress, in the same way that,
say, you wouldn't let foreigners see round certain areas of
your factory. If Peter was humiliated and ashamed by my
bumbling performance in the 800 metres, he had reason to
be, but he should have been more discreet. What he said
was the sort of direct thing that comes naturally to him, and
I wouldn't try to change a man of sixty. But people just
didn't understand. When a coach has given twelve years
driving towards a peak, and an athlete of my standing
then runs so ineptly, the coach *is* going to feel slightly
humiliated. But his reaction in public added to the illusion
that I do only what I am told, that he puts the boot in,

that he has no feeling for me, and that it was he who had been hurt. People can only equate our relationship with their own with their fathers. Maybe some of the people who were heavy on Peter had a distant or unsatisfactory relationship with their fathers. He brought the trouble on himself after the 800 metres by his open frankness, his choice of adjectives, but as he said to me after the severe press reaction, 'I suppose they just don't understand'. If I'd failed again in the 1,500 metres, we'd both have got a lot more stick. Other coaches spend as much time or more with their athletes, but they don't get the same criticism if the athlete loses. It was crazy, for instance, that the consensus of opinion after Prague was that Peter had lost me the race.

Climbing up out of Sheffield on the A57 towards Glossop and Manchester, past the neat semis and bungalows with their tidy front gardens in the only conservative constituency in South Yorkshire, the road winds down again before rising past the Howden reservoirs to Hollow Meadows. Cocooned in the driver's car, the harsh April wind outside, which rips across the barren moors, seems no inconvenience. Eventually we come to a turning on the right. It is the start of a ten mile run across some of the most exposed country in England. A farmer in gaiters is busily unconcerned in his barn, with its leaning, undulating roof. As we pull up in the loose stones on the edge of the unfenced road, a sheep dog bounds across and barks at us because there is nothing better to do. The runner gets out of the front passenger seat in his track-suit, and the east wind grabs at the open door. The driver checks the stop watch round his neck and the runner sets off across the moonscape. It takes him the first mile to pick up his rhythm, to begin to get really warm, and as we climb, the speedometer hovering around 10 m.p.h. in second gear, the view of the reservoirs opens up far below. The heather and last year's matted, crumbling bracken are now almost head high on the steep banks as the runner starts to push harder and the driver has to accelerate to keep pace. There is not a soul in sight, just the occasional morose looking ewe nibbling away at dead pasture as appetizing as a scrubbing brush. The driver glances at the watch and gives a nod of approval. The real destination is still a long way off; but it is up here, far from the omnivorous eye of television, that the critical work is done. The driver says, 'the danger is of being complacent, to let it become easy, but at the back of your mind you know that other lonely men around the world are grinding it out just like this'.

Following a few yards behind, one becomes mesmerized by the clockwork motion of the slim figure pounding away over the tarmac, leaning into the head wind. A thin sun comes through the cloud, and you hope that some of the warmth is reflected onto the runner off the high stone wall which now skirts the road. 'He always drives hard into the inclines, then takes it easy down hill', says the man at the wheel, hunching forward as if to try to help the runner. 'It's so tempting to do it the other way round, to go easy up the hills, then open out when the gradient flattens.' The road now runs through a little sheltered niche between the hills, with ivy and bramble tumbling over the high walls. The route twists and turns downwards again towards the village of Low Bradfield, and now the runner is really flowing at well under six minutes to the mile.

We glide through the village, past the pub and the post office, and the green with its cricket square in roped-off cold storage. A woman with a shopping basket turns to her companion with a nudge which says, 'it's him'. We turn round the end of the reservoir, alongside the pines which fringe the water. A couple of crews, also out training, rest gratefully on their sixteen oars, their eyes devouring in unison the figure flitting so swiftly past the trees, oblivious momentarily of their own objectives as they study someone whose destiny has these past months been the discussion of almost every sportsman in the land. The road climbs again, up past smarter houses now, and the next mile slips by in a little over five minutes. Eventually we pull up outside a pub, the ten mile mark, not an oasis of respite. The runner walks back to the car breathing

hard but not in discomfort, and rests his head on his arms
on the car roof. The driver winds down the window and
puts a fond hand on the pale blue tracksuit to measure
and record the heart-beat. They exchange a smile and the
runner says simply, 'that was good'. He has done it a
hundred times before, but each time the experience is different. Today the wind made it particularly hard, but both
the runner and the driver know that things are going well.

═══════════

    ❝I've trained over the peaks from the age of eleven
or twelve. Often I was running with senior athletes and
I have always enjoyed it, the loneliness, the solitude up
among the pine forests on a Sunday morning. I find the remoteness up there so stimulating, especially when there is a
white-out and there are no other cars about. Some days,
when Sheffield and Manchester are cut off from each
other by snow, there's a sense of total isolation only a few
miles from the house. The weather in the winter is so
uncertain, it can be really cutting when the fog and ice
close in. I've been out on occasions wearing three tracksuits and a waterproof. On some runs I've come back with
my eyelashes frozen. The day before Christmas last
winter it was really miserable when I did fourteen or fifteen miles and I came back drenched through. In a running family, that's business as usual. But whatever the
weather, it's always exhilarating in a funny sort of way,
the challenge of beating the elements.

    I would do it even if I was not aiming for the Olympics
or world records. It's something which most of my friends
who have quit racing do regularly on a Sunday. It's difficult to describe why, unless you've been up there and
come round the shoulder of a hill, and there suddenly is
the whole of Sheffield laid out miles below. I've never felt
frustrated up there the way I have working on the track,
because up there you are surrounded by beauty. I always
think it is silly the way the north of England is so badly
promoted by the situation comedies on television, the
image of Coronation Street and satanic mills, when we

have so much beauty so close to the people in the northern cities. *

======

Almost the only flat stretch of road around Sheffield runs
through the Rivelin Valley, between precipitous farm
land on one side and wooded hills and allotments on the
other. Alongside the road, hidden among trees, is a stream
and a protected nature walk. It is along this road, a fraction over three miles before it hits the city near the Sheffield Wednesday football ground, that some of the most
remarkable runs of all time have been made, observed
only by mothers with prams and a few disinterested
motorists. Along this stretch it is possible to fit in six consecutive half-miles, and it is these sequences that have built in
Seb the exceptional stamina which, until a couple of years
ago, none but Peter knew he possessed. So impressive
were the figures, so revealing of the young student's
potential, that he and his coach resisted all requests to
come and film him in action. It is here that the positions
of runner and driver are reversed, with Peter moving
ahead to pace his athlete, and draw him out occasionally
to some quite exceptional times. On one of the days when
I was there he did a sequence of six, with recovery intervals of only a minute and a half between each, and the
third of the series was almost fast enough to qualify for
the semi-final of the 800 metres in one of the six first-
round heats in Moscow. 'He's feeling rather pleased with
himself, and he's entitled to', observed Peter, as we pulled
up at the finish of the series near a bus stop of afternoon
giggling schoolgirls. They didn't recognize the slim young
man standing there on the pavement with heaving chest.
Just another of those funny joggers they thought, no
doubt, as they stared a trifle embarrassed. Within two
minutes of the finish of this gruelling session Seb's pulse
rate was back down to only 86, and off he went on a
two-mile warm-down. The ring-master was pleased. He'd
gently needled the performer before the start about
whether he was in shape.

That was no breach of their trust. Peter said:

'I've never ever told him a false time to encourage him. Whoever beats him is going to know he has been in a race. I may not be the best coach in the world, but what I am doing for Seb is right – which is not to say someone else might not do it better. It's true that I came to it fresh, that I wasn't conditioned by training dogmas handed down through the generations. Because I was so involved with him, people thought we must be doing a hundred miles a week, when in fact we were doing under thirty when he came third in Athens in the European Junior. There is nothing basically wrong with a parent being a coach, though I have seen many kids damaged by their fathers trying to overcome their own deficiencies through the child's achievements. What has helped, though it may sound élitist, is an intelligent approach to the problems. Mechanical engineering has actually been a help, too, in bringing him through his adolescence. Running, in my opinion, is to a great extent science-based, but it is also an art, because science does not offer all the answers. Managing an engineering business successfully demands co-ordination in a whole range of aspects. To get something done, you call upon the best resources. When I came into athletics I didn't know much about physiology, but I knew of people who did. There was any amount of advice, but so much of it conflicting. So I did a lot of reading and went to conferences and listened to a lot of people – and discarded much of what I read and heard. I discovered what Astrand, the Swedish sports physiologist, and the German Gerschler had written. But I realized that nobody actually *knew* for sure. There is nothing revolutionary in what I have done with Seb, but it has been tailor-made for his physique. An athlete to a great extent determines his own training by his responses to the tasks you set for him and by his racing results. The coach must adjust to the athlete.

'Seb is not a mindless automaton who would go out and run unquestioningly, but I have had to be certain that he would adhere to the programme when I was not there, yet that he would vary it when necessary because of the weather. He is exceptional because his trust in me is total. The coach can only work with the athlete's consent. The measure of the athlete is the extent of his consenting to do things within his capacity. But the danger for the coach is that if the athlete's trust is total, he may consent to anything.

'In conversation with other coaches, I've not heard of one athlete who is as dedicated as Seb though, admittedly, I don't know all the athletes abroad, and one knows that some in the past such as Elliott trained phenomenally hard. I'm far from perfect and, although Seb says he gets on well with me, I think his going to Loughborough was important. The strain of eating and sleeping under the same roof over the last four years, at the same time as the racing pressure on him increased, too, might have become too much. Yet we have only had one serious disagreement and that was before his world records, but it had nothing to do with athletics. Events really began to change with the sudden acceleration of Seb's progress in the summer of 1979, though how much this was a result of relief at getting his degree it would be hard to say. Certainly it came a year earlier than I had reckoned. I expected him to get down *near* Juantorena's 800 metres world record of 1:43·4, maybe clip a bit off by September, but not take a whole second off in July! Possibly what pleased me most was that he did it on his own, and I sensed a qualitative change in his make-up. My real joy was not only the record, but that it was one in the eye for all those who suggested he couldn't do anything without his Dad. I can't break any records, but what I can say is that I have managed to produce a runner in the round.

'Of course his three world records were a triumph and of course I had some reflected glory, but coaching someone from youth is all about weaning. The athlete should be coach-orientated, but should not become coach-dependent. My success was that he went out to Oslo for the 800 metres, assessed the situation, picked

up the 'phone and said, "this is what I think". He had
gone there with instructions to win a tactical race. I said,
"if what you tell me is correct, then go for the time
instead of the win". You teach an athlete to train as
much as to race. When he went to the front 450 metres
from the finish of the Oslo Golden Mile it was the sign
of an intelligent runner. He was in unknown territory,
and he'd only run a handful of four-lap races, but his
instinct told him to capitalize on his strength at that
moment. I'd told him the tactics would probably be dic-
tated to him, but he suddenly knew he had to make the
decisions.'

===========

‘I suppose you could say my father could now die
a happy man. He's seen the satisfactory culmination of
twelve years' work, and certainly he'll retire the day I quit.
He's done what he set out to do, and from now on it can
no longer be the same. We talked about it quite a bit
before the Games, knowing that his role would change
quite considerably from now on. I sense for him, as for
me, that while there is still a lot to go for – world records
and medals – they can never produce the same feeling as
the first time. He's quite sentimental at heart, more than
you'd suppose. A year ago or so Kenny Moore, the
American marathon runner and writer for *Sports Illustrated*, was staying with us, and talked about giving us a
dog. Peter was quite put out. 'There's no way he's going
to pull that one on us, we'll have no bloody animal in this
house.' On Christmas Eve, Kenny turned up on the
doorstep with a small round puppy wagging its tail, and
Peter just looked at it and said, 'Oh, well. What are we
going to call it?'›

3 : Rivalry

The 1977 edition of *Athletics* – that excellent annual fund
of information and statistics edited by Ron Pickering and
Mel Watman – contained no entry for Sebastian Coe
under its section 'Who's Who in the British team', for the
good reason that he was not in the team the previous season when only nineteen. Steve Ovett, on the other hand,
born a year earlier than Coe in 1955 in Brighton, merited
an entry of eleven lines. He had won the 1973 European
Junior 800 metres and a silver medal a year later, aged
nineteen, among the seniors in Rome. In 1975 he won the
Europa Cup 800 metres, was a disappointed fifth off the
outside lane in the Montreal Olympics, and was unquestionably the golden boy of British middle distance running. With a build almost four inches taller than Coe, at 6
feet 1 inch, and 25 pounds heavier at 11 stone, he was,
for traditionalists, the 'good big 'un' who would always
beat the 'good little 'un'. The emergence of a young student from Loughborough, whose academic schedule post-
poned the start of his serious racing season until the
middle of each summer, posed little threat to the sump-
tuously equipped former art student from Brighton. Or did it?

❝I first realized that from Steve's point of view I
was more than just another rival at the end of the 1977

season, which was my first major outdoor season. Little
comments had come my way. For instance, when asked
what he thought of my prospects, he thought I would
'never be fast enough to run a really world class 800
metres'. It was only a few weeks after that remark that I
broke Andy Carter's U.K. record, running second behind
Mike Boit in the Coca-Cola at Crystal Palace, and being
the first Briton under 1:45, with 1:44·95. I always had the
feeling that when the gap began to disappear – Steve's
best up to then was 1:45·4 – the rivalry would become
greater, and with it his need to prove himself. To an
extent, of course, it did us both good. Sport thrives on
rivalry and colour. Bayi v Walker had been a huge talking
point leading up to the Montreal Olympics and then, sadly,
never occurred because of the African boycott. But, as
with Ryun v Keino, Pirie v Kuts, or Bannister v Landy,
they were not from the same country. The *real* intensity
occurs when you get two men from the same country, such
as Hägg and Andersson, who broke each other's 1,500
metres and mile records eight times between 1941 and
1945. What has made it so interesting in the case of Steve
and me, I feel, is that we are both so different, not just
physically but in attitudes, too. After my record in the
Coke I was surprised when Steve, who was the fellow with
the reputation, ignored me in the warm-up area. Dave
Jenkins said to me, 'he's like that'. I wondered why.❜

———————

The previous season, 1976, in which Seb and his coach
had decided that they must move away from the 5,000
metres and concentrate on basic speed, Seb was running
experimentally in the main. In the Kraft Games, bidding
for Olympic selection, in his own opinion he had run
badly in the 1,500 metres, in spite of a personal best of
3:43·2, finishing seventh. There had been another hassle
with the authorities because he was in the middle of
exams and had trouble getting to Crystal Palace on time.
In the AAA final, after only three weeks' serious training,
he improved his time marginally with 3:42·6, to finish

fourth behind Dixon, Moorcroft, and Clement, beating off a challenge from Quax. The next week at Gateshead, running in gale conditions and setting the pace from the front, he finished third in the mile behind Walker and Moorcroft. Back at Crystal Palace, still experimenting, he led for three laps in the Emsley Carr Mile, was brushed aside on the final bend by Malinowski's elbow, and faded on the run in to finish seventh, in spite of beating four minutes for the first time with 3:58·3. Moorcroft won a fine race from Bayi.

———

❝I particularly wanted to get under four minutes, so I had to run from the front to extend myself. I had nothing to learn from hanging back among the pack. Peter and I had always believed, even when I was younger, that it was important to go out and *commit* yourself, it is the only way to find out about yourself and others. If I'd sat with the pack I would have been out-kicked even earlier, finishing outside four minutes, and learning nothing . . . except that I hadn't got a kick, as yet. I was encouraged a lot by these races and it was now, during the winter at Loughborough, that I began to gain the benefit of the speed and weight training with George. He made me a lot stronger. I ventured into my first indoor track 'season', ran a 600 metres before Christmas in 1:19·7, and won the U.K. Indoor 800 metres in 1:49·1, my first senior title. I was really beginning to feel in control of my strength and my legs, and followed it up with the 800 metres U.K. record against Germany in Dortmund, and a Commonwealth indoor record of 1:47·5, against France at Cosford, leading all the way.❞

———

It was a small British team spearheaded by Seb which went to the European Indoor Championships in San Sebastian in 1977. We flew to Bilbao, and thence took a mini-bus to San Sebastian's picturesque bay. Seb and I

chatted on the way out, and shortly afterwards he was
surprised when he was given a stern warning by the formidable Marea Hartman that he would be well advised,
for reasons about which she was not specific, to steer well
clear of both me and Ron Pickering. Some of those with
administrative power in amateur sport and who, in their
honorary positions, in many instances enjoy a status which
far exceeds that of their daily working or social life, do
not take kindly to the enquiring eye and ear of the media.

It was a memorable occasion for both Seb and young
Katrina Colebrook, coached by their father and mother
respectively, each winning the 800 metres. Katrina slaugh-
tered the combined might of Eastern Europe to equal the
world best of 2:1·1, while Seb, leading from gun to tape,
was a tenth of a second outside the Italian Carlo
Grippo's world record with 1:46·5.

―――――――

❝I was on cloud nine, and I felt I had every right
to be. With no international experience until two weeks
before, I had won a European title. Peter was delighted
that I had done it on my own and had run from the front,
but I must admit that the tactics were partly inspired by
some lurid stories from the knowledgeable Cliff Temple of
The Sunday Times, who had opened my eyes with his
description of blood all over the boards from ripped tendons. I was also amused and surprised by my first experience of British management abroad. Our manager was the
amiable, avuncular Bob Stinson, a former Achilles runner.
He has recently done valuable work in formulating British
proposals to the International Federation aimed at
rationalizing the anomalies of so-called amateur athletics.
But he was an exceedingly low-key manager! While other
coaches were rushing around shouting, Stinson simply
looked at me rather balefully when the time came for me
to leave the warm-up area and go out for the final, and his
only comment was 'well, bye-bye then'. In fact, I quite
like that kind of detachment, I don't want instructions or
advice from any official other than my coach.

Ten days later I damaged an achilles tendon and was out of action for fourteen weeks; not running again until July in one of Geoff Capes's enjoyable Dewhurst meetings at Spalding. I came second in the AAA 800 metres behind Savic of Yugoslavia, running well above my level of fitness, to beat that big-hearted competitor Walker with 1:46·8. Against expectation, in view of my injury, I was selected for the Europa Cup Final in Helsinki. **)**

There was an outside hope that, if everything went well, Britain might have ousted one of the East European state 'machines', Russia or East Germany, for a place in the eight-nation World Cup, due to take place in Düsseldorf. In the event, both men's and women's teams performed satisfactorily to come fourth and third respectively. But the men's 800 metres was a farce. Running wide off the final bend and making ground fast on the leaders, Seb was disgracefully given a short-arm tackle by Willy Wulbeck as the West German suddenly switched lanes from the inside and went on to win in 1:47·21. After losing several strides, Seb finished fourth behind Beyer of East Germany and Marajo of France. Wulbeck should certainly have been disqualified for an outrageous foul, but the appeal jury rejected Britain's immediate protest even after looking at the video recording. It was Seb's first bad international experience.

(I was reluctant at the time to say so, it sounded presumptuous, but I felt I had been going to win because I had just gone past Wulbeck and was gaining on the others. But I was a real novice, it was my first senior out-door international and I was taken aback by such tactics. I felt awful about it afterwards, both shins had been spiked and the *Daily Telegraph* didn't help matters by saying that I 'appeared to stumble'. I ran the five miles back to the hall of residence thinking that if I had been fit enough I

could have gone to the front earlier. It had no lasting significance, however, other than the lingering doubt at the
back of my mind that I was vulnerable to the hand-off,
and that winter I stepped up my weight training with
George.

Two days later I was in Brussels for the Ivo Van
Damme Memorial, and ran a personal best of 1:46·3 to
take third place in the 800 metres behind Boit and
Enyeart. Running against West Germany at Crystal Palace
a week later I won the 800 metres and, as I was leaving
the stadium, I was asked by Brian Hewson and Mike Farrell, the organizers, if I would run the Emsley Carr Mile
the next day. One of the Sunday papers said it was a
'reward' from the British Board, but the fact was there
was no one else.*

───────────

Out-kicking Bayi in the final straight for a sub-56 last
quarter-mile, Seb recorded 3:57·7 to become the youngest
winner of the event, though it is interesting to reflect that
his time, run at the age of twenty, would be substantially
improved by teenagers Graham Williamson and Steve
Cram within the next three years. It was the first time that
Seb had earned a back-page headline, with the *Mirror*'s
'Bold King Coe' on the Monday morning. Yet although
Coe had now gained the U.K. record at 800 metres in the
Coke, Ovett held both the 1,500 metres and the mile,
with Seb not even ranked in the U.K. all-time top ten. His
rise had passed largely unnoticed in academic circles at
Loughborough, too. When a BBC film crew enquired if
they could set up a unit to film a sequence of Sebastian
Coe in the library, the librarian queried, 'do you mean
the one who comes in here on Friday mornings to read
Athletics Weekly?'

Early in 1978 he suffered a serious injury, putting his
foot down an old gate-post hole while out training at
Loughborough, was lucky not to break the ankle, and
severely ruptured all the tendons. He sat in agony while
his sock expanded like a balloon as he watched it. He

crawled across the field to a security car that happened to
be there on the campus and was rushed to hospital by
George.

―――――――

‘I was carried pick-a-back 200 yards from the car
park to Casualty, where it was the usual Sunday scene:
kids who'd fallen off swings at the playground, etc. ... I
sat with my leg in a sling for an hour and eventually was
taken to the X-ray department, where the Sister said it
was broken. George insisted it wasn't. Sister: 'I'm telling
you it is.' George: 'I'm not a betting man' (which was a
bare-faced lie because he would bet on two earwigs climbing a wall), 'but I'll put my shirt on it that it's not.' Sister:
'What are your qualifications?' George: 'MSc in bio-
mechanics.' Whereupon she immediately started calling
him 'Dad'. The X-ray attendant cheerfully volunteered:
'It's so bad that if it's not broken, it would be better if it
was!' The Sister now insisted it should be put in plaster.
George: 'No, there'll be muscle wastage and we won't be
able to give him physiotherapy.' Sister: 'Get out of here at
once.' I was wheeled towards the plaster room. George:
'Do you realize you are dealing with the fastest 800
metre runner in the world?' Defiant Sister: 'Well, he'll just
have to be the slowest for a change.'

I sat there listening to this row as if it was all happening
to somebody else. George promptly discharged me, and
the sequel was that when we saw a consultant the following morning, Peter having come down from Sheffield, the
Sister threatened to report George to the Medical Council
for impersonating my father – which of course he hadn't.
The consultant insisted that it would take me six months
to recover, but I went to see George Preston, a marvellous
physiotherapist who used to be with Leicester City F.C.,
and within ten days I was jogging again, which tells you a
lot about the quality of sports medicine in general practice
in Britain.

Initially I was running in intense pain – the only time
we have ever hurried an injury. I lost about a month of

flat-out preparation, and then went on holiday with the
family to the Adriatic, where it was really too hot for
training and my weight went down a stone to only 8·5 –
the result of trying to do too much too quickly. Peter
worked brilliantly to get me back into some sort of shape
for the selection trials for the European Championships.
We'd previously decided that I would not attempt the
Commonwealth Games, that the real challenge would lie
in Prague. I managed to win the selection race, the U.K.
Championships at Meadowbank, after being disqualified
initially for breaking lane too early at the end of the stag-
ger. I hadn't.**

A fortnight before going to Prague for the European
Championships, Seb was at his favourite Van Damme
meeting in Brussels, lowering his own 800 metres U.K.
record to 1:44·3 ahead of American James Robinson and
Marajo of France. A first lap of 50·5 showed that he'd got
back much of the lost ground and, remarkably, he was now
getting within range of Juantorena's record of 1:43·4.
Moreover, as he set off for Prague it was with the knowledge that he was now the fastest in Europe and almost
two seconds inside Ovett's best time to date, his 1:45·4 in
1976. But Seb soon ran into problems.

**Prague was cold, wet and wretched. The accom-
modation was gloomy, the food was poor and unappetiz-
ing, and many of the team went down with a stomach bug.
I was one of them and, with my weight *already* down to
eight stone, it further drained my strength. In addition, I
was quickly to discover that some athletes were more
equal than others as far as the British Board were concerned. Not only had I been obliged to run in the trials
where others had been excused, in spite of the fact that I
was ranked first in Europe, but I was further annoyed to
find that Steve was being allowed to postpone his decision

on whether he would run the 800 metres in addition to the 1,500 metres right up to the last minute. Within what was supposed to be a team this was clearly unfair on the guy who was number one on times, but needed help in his first championships. Steve was saying he'd decide three or four hours before his heat, and the Board allowed him to play a psychological game with another member of the team. It's nice, even necessary, to know what you've got to face so that you can plan, though it doesn't bother me the same now. Steve appeared to try it again over Moscow, saying well on into the summer that he had a moral dilemma over Afghanistan, and that he didn't know if he would run; but I was sure he would. I'm not saying it would have made any difference to the situation if I had known in Prague whether he was running or not, but it would have reduced the pressure on me. The Board have never taken a strong line with him. To make matters worse, Harry Wilson, who was national coach for middle distances and was out there in that capacity with the team, was also Steve's personal coach and spent much of the time out of the village with Steve in an official car which was supposed to be available to all. On the night before the 800 metres final, Wilson was overheard on the stairs in the village saying to another athlete, 'as far as I'm concerned, there's no way Coe can beat Steve tomorrow'. In Prague he was officially as much my coach as Steve's, although of course Peter was out there with me. **)**

Both runners cruised through their semi-finals, Coe in 1:47·6, Ovett in 1:46·5. Juantorena, there as a guest of his European 'brothers', said before the final: 'At this moment I think it will be Coe – but we ought to wait and see.' Reckoning that his chances depended on a scorching first leg which might drain Ovett, Seb went through the first lap in a blistering 49·3, the swiftest ever run. Down the back straight he held his lead, with Ovett tucked in behind and then the East German Olaf Beyer, a twenty-one-year-old maths student from Potsdam. As they came off the final bend Ovett pounced to overtake the now fading Seb – but he had been trailing the wrong man. Fifty yards from the tape Beyer edged past Ovett and the British pair, who had been regarded as certainties throughout Europe for the first two places, had to settle for silver and bronze. Ovett's 1:44·1 lowered Coe's two-week-old record, and Beyer's 1:43·8 was the fifth fastest of all time and a tenth outside the Italian Fiasconaro's European record. There was no sign of Ovett's by now famous wave as he covered his face with his hands in dismay. He then refused to attend the official Czech press conference, saying he had no need of 'useless publicity'.

‹The extraordinary thing about Beyer was that Steve and I didn't see him again for ages. As he ran through the finishing line he was wrapped in blankets by two officials and hurried from the arena, instead of going off on a lap of honour, as you would expect from someone who had just won a European title. Geoff Capes and Dave Jenkins say that he walked off with his eyes completely slack. And he then went missing. We were informed that he'd provided his urine sample within thirteen minutes of running 1:43, which is unusual to say the least. It took Steve and me almost an hour and a half, and we only saw Beyer again at the victory ceremony.›

Such is the widespread incidence of the use of stimulants, particularly in the United States and Eastern Europe, that suspicions inevitably arise when an athlete behaves as strangely as Beyer did in Prague.

‹It had always been my intention to run from the front; Peter and I wanted to test the concept that no one can kick off sub-1:44 pace, or even sub-1:45. And it proved it. What happened was that I slowed the most, then Steve, with Beyer managing to sustain his speed that little bit longer. Approaching world record pace it comes down to who fades the least. Kicking is not a last 200 metres in 26, it's in 23. A 26 is just maintaining your form. In that race, the guy who did the least for most of the race was first and I did the most and was third. Brendan Foster had agreed with my plan, saying, 'right, even if you risk failing, do it that way'. Most people thought I was nuts, though Adrian Metcalfe was one of the few who had anything good to say: 'I take my hat off to anyone who has the guts to go out and run in a championship at that initial pace.' Steve said afterwards that he reckoned that if he'd made his effort at 200 metres instead of 90 he might have won, but I feel that at the pace of that race he would have simply faded earlier.

Both Peter and I thought that a sub-50 first lap would be possible at some future date when I was fit. People were inclined to forget that Prague was my first championship with heats and semi-finals, and there was the fact that my weight was seriously down and my ankle was swelling after every run. The thing about athletics is that it is like poker sometimes: you know what's in your hand, and it may be a load of old rubbish, but you have to keep up a front! I went to Prague hoping to make the most of the psychological advantage of my time in Brussels, but knowing that it was not really representative of what I was consistently capable of at that time. The lesson Prague really taught me was never again to reckon on only one opponent in the field. Somewhere at this very moment, training far away from the sophisticated media and without all the pressures, there's probably someone running at altitude in Kenya or Mexico who is suddenly going to appear out of the blue, and we will know very little about him. That is great – as it should be. 9

Peter looks for the iron in a runner. 'I want to see what the bastards are made of' he said before the race. My

opinion is that the result in Prague did more than
anything, when the time came, to persuade Peter and Seb
not to run from the front in Moscow – when the
justification for doing so was in fact far greater. It is
significant that Peter said to me after Prague not only that
he had learned much about reactions to world record
pace, but that front running would always be risky and
that the man with the basic speed would always be safer
running from the back. Peter:

> 'Seb had, and still has, the ability and the bravery to do
> whatever is necessary to learn and improve, whatever
> the cost at the time. He could have blamed Prague on
> me, but in spite of being miserable he did not then or
> subsequently ever reproach me. He was in there to
> apply maximum pressure on others and that's what he
> did. The result wasn't bad for a part-timer in the fifth
> fastest race ever. We had already decided that for
> 1979–80 he would become full-time, we knew that in
> 1978 he was nowhere near the limit of his training
> schedules.'

‘After Prague I reckoned it would do me good to
run a two miles in the Coca-Cola to end off the season.
Brendan, who has been a very good friend and counsellor,
had thought it was a good idea, too, but in Prague, before
we left, Alan Pascoe came up to me and told me I was
down for the 800 metres. I said I wanted the two miles
but Andy Norman, the Southern Counties AAA official
who has done an enormous amount to help promote
sponsored international meetings in Britain and is now an
international selector, told me that the 800 metres was
going to be very good, with both Wulbeck and Boit in the
field. But they both pulled out before the day, and
Norman subsequently told Brendan that I had been kept
out of the two miles because Steve didn't want me in the
race. I felt flattered. The 800 metres ended up being a
totally domestic affair, and I managed to get back the

U.K. record from Steve, being the first Briton under 1:44
with 1:43·95 ahead of Dane Joseph. Again Steve ignored
me after the record that night, and Peter couldn't resist
quipping to Harry Wilson before we left the stadium:
'Congratulate Steve on his two mile record, but just tell
him we always considered the 800 metres record was only
borrowed!'
   The same night Steve had set a world two mile best of
8:13·5, beating Brendan's record, and in the process he
defeated the sensational Henry Rono, who that year had
established a unique quartet of world records at 3,000
metres, 5,000 metres, 10,000 metres, and the 3,000
metres steeplechase. But Steve treated him shoddily when
he was tired, coming level with him in the finishing
straight, giving him a stare, and then waving as if to say
goodbye as he sprinted for the tape. I really cannot
condone so much of Steve's behaviour on and off the
track. He is without question a wonderful athlete and my
admiration of him as such is sincere and unbounded, but
he does conduct himself in a way which regularly leaves so
much to be desired. He should not belittle inferior opponents in lesser races the way he sometimes does. That is
sheer bad manners.'

—————

Ovett's progress, the Prague 800 metres disappointment
apart, had continued to be spectacular over four laps.
Winning the Europa Cup 1,500 metres in Helsinki in
1977, then the World Cup in Düsseldorf with a U.K.
record of 3:34·5 ahead of Wessinghage (West Germany)
and Straub (GDR), with Walker sadly failing to finish,
and then in Prague he had imperiously won the 1,500
metres in a championship record of 3:35·6 ahead of
Coghlan (Eire) and Commonwealth champion Moorcroft.

—————

'Many athletes can't help feeling that Steve has
had kid-glove treatment from the Board. When he left the

British team in the middle of a two-day match with West
Germany in Bremen to go and run in Nijmegen in
Holland, he received only a mild reprimand, whereas
Jenkins in similar circumstances, running abroad without
formal clearance, was suspended from international
competition. On the second day why shouldn't Steve
support those in the team who had supported him on the
first? I can begin to understand his attitude towards the
press, it's his business whether he talks to them or not, but
I can't understand his attitude to other athletes. How
could he claim before the Golden Mile in Oslo in 1979
that the race would be 'hollow' without him, that he had
no need to pursue the other top milers around the world
when he had nothing to prove? I still somehow expected
him to turn up, but I was already beginning not to care. If
he did, he did. I'd had a conversation with his father at
Crystal Palace before going to Oslo, he'd been very
pleasant to me out in Prague. I asked him whether Steve
was running in Oslo or not, and he replied, 'from what I
understand, he isn't'. Poor fellow, I thought to myself, you
know as much as I do. After I broke the mile record in
Oslo, Steve said, when asked whether he would congratulate me, 'why should I, it's not my record. I don't
get caught up in times. I never run against the clock. I run
against men on the day.'❜

———

Ovett had expressly stated that he would make 1979 a
quiet year, prior to the Olympics, but John Rodda, the
respected writer of the *Guardian*, felt obliged to say after
the Golden Mile that 'Ovett must really eat those words
about the victory in the race he missed being hollow'.

———

❛I'd taken Steve's words at face value. What he
said about a quiet year made sense after two or three hard
seasons, why should he extend himself in the pre-Olympic
year? For myself, I thought the international competition

would do me good, though from the outset I made it clear
I was willing to run for Britain in the Europa Cup semi-
final and final, but did not wish to be selected for the
World Cup in Montreal.

Steve had said so often, in *Athletics Weekly* and
elsewhere, that world records didn't interest him, that all
he cared about was winning races. When I set the world
records in 1979 he said dismissively that if that was what
gave me pleasure, it was up to me. Yet by August he had
a carefully orchestrated record-breaking circus on the road
with the help of Andy Norman. It seemed that my records
forced him to break cover. He'd never previously exposed
himself, running tactical races from the back to win in
around 3:35/3:37. Steve's attitude to record breaking in
1979–80 has taken much of the romance and the
unexpected element out of the sport. His two runs in
Brussels were like moon-shots, Steve, the rocket, shedding
pace-makers like bits of equipment all the way, until only
the 'lunar module' was left to attempt the final 'landing'. I
have never transported a clique of pace-makers with me
when attempting records, and I have only ever made three
deliberate record attempts – the 1,500 metres in Zürich in
1979 and 1980 and the 1,000 metres in Oslo in 1980 –
and in none of them did I know who was going to be
making the pace. When I set the record in 1979 in Zürich
I had to run the last two laps on my own, and for the 800
metres and mile records in Oslo there was no pacing
specifically planned for me. **)**

━━━━━━━

There is no doubt that at various times over recent years
Ovett has exerted an influence on the composition of the
field for races in which he would run. The most bizarre
was in 1977 at Crystal Palace, when Juantorena would
not run against Ovett, and Ovett would not run against
Boit, so that Boit finished up running an almost
meaningless 800 metres B race without serious opposition.
Steve Scott, the American who finished second to Coe in
the 1979 Golden Mile, insists that Ovett twice avoided

him in early season races in 1980 in the States: 'Any
conversation with Steve about athletics is shallow, because
I can never be sure of what he is saying.' The BBC were
left in no doubt, however, when Ovett informed them that
he would only attend their 1980 Sportsview Personality of
the Year award programme 'if I am the winner'. In the
event Seb was the runner-up to ice-skater Robin Cousins.

━━━━━━━

     ‘ It was silly when Steve tried to contrive a pre-
Olympic ‘challenge’ with me when he came back from the
States in early 1980. I first heard about it on the radio
coming out of Trent Bridge after watching cricket on a
Sunday. I’d already agreed with Andy Norman to run for
England at Crystal Palace in the Bannister Mile within the
England–Belgium–Scotland match because Steve *wanted*
the 800 metres. He knew perfectly well that in an
Olympic year it would do neither of us any good to get
caught up in a really fast race against each other so early
in the season. He’d heard I’d pulled out of a race at
Loughborough because of a hamstring strain, so he tried
to switch to the mile and persuade the AAA, through
Norman, that it would be a good thing. It was just sheer
opportunism because he happened to be ready earlier. He
had already beaten Scott and Bayi, and if he now beat me
he could have gone to the Olympics with the psychological
advantage of having already beaten the main contenders –
though in the event Scott didn’t go because of the boycott
and Bayi ran the 3,000 metres.
    Steve really isn’t very shrewd with many of his public
comments. When he was asked if he would be going
abroad for winter training before the Olympics he said he
wouldn’t because he was too patriotic! He should try coming to train up in Sheffield or Newcastle in the winter with
me or Bren, when you often can’t get the car out for days
at a time because of the snow. It’s not quite like that in
Brighton. He has accused me of being a ‘programmed’
athlete, but every world class athlete has a programme, as
he well knows, and mine has been designed to allow me to

study at the same time. Often when he makes a comment in public it turns out to be a good omen for me. He said I would never run a fast 800 metres, that the Golden Mile would be hollow, that he had a ninety per cent chance in the Olympic 1,500 metres, and, after his world record 1,500 metres of 3:31·4 in Koblenz in 1980, that only he and Wessinghage were 'capable of beating 3:30'. I just hoped then that time would prove him wrong! Yet these criticisms relate to behaviour, and I would never for a moment detract from his enormous athletic talent and unparalleled record of racing achievement. In this capacity he has been at the forefront of the resurgence in British athletics.'

4:Forty-one Days

The winter of 1978–9 was endlessly depressing, an expanse of fog and ice and little daylight, the evenings seeming to begin soon after lunch. For Seb, who had stepped up his winter work to around seventy miles a week for the first time, it required an iron will to maintain his schedules, training early each morning, and again in the evening after a day spent studying for his economics degree. Often he would be running by the light of the moon on snow-covered pavements, foot-paths and lanes, every stride a potential hazard. Only somebody with his extraordinarily detached, clear-sighted view of his objectives could have endured all those hours in which the horizon never came any nearer. One evening towards the end of the winter he was out on a ten-mile run with a couple of Yorkshire colleagues, Malcolm Prince and Andy Armitage. He covered ten miles in three quarters of an hour (the 10-mile world record of Jos Hermens of Holland is 45:57·2), an average of just over 4:30 to the mile, at the end of which he was sick. He went back to his digs, changed, and went to a reception being given by the university warden. After two glasses of wine he felt his legs going, slumped to the floor, and woke up the next day back at his digs where his colleagues had taken him. An Olympic athlete's social life is not a merry one. His April and May appointments were primarily with the 400 metres, working his time down to around 47 seconds in a succession of college meetings, with a relay leg of 46·3. These, you might say, were his 'May Ball'.

_____

‘My premier aim in 1979 was to get a degree, everything else was subordinate to that. Looking back, 1979 was no different from the year before or the year before that: a reduction in training from March onwards, exams in June, and then a build up of training again afterwards. Peter, George Gandy and I looked at the situation and calculated that if things went well I might get down to somewhere near the pace for a world record 800 metres by the Zürich meeting in the middle of August. I finished exams in the middle of June and caught a virus soon afterwards, probably because I was run down and very tired. Suddenly having nothing to concentrate on, I found myself falling asleep at odd moments and I went to Malmo for the semi-final of the Europa Cup against a background of immensely thorough preparation over many months but in need of sharpening up. It was, in fact, one of the best trips I have ever been on. A lot of senior athletes had turned down the invitation: Geoff Capes, Dave Moorcroft, Brian Hooper and I were the four most senior people there; the team spirit was tremendous, with field events men shouting for the 10,000 metres runners and vice versa. And we were all astonished by the prices out there. After buying a bottle of coke and a tooth-brush I'd just about exhausted the Board's spending allowance for the three days.

I'd withdrawn from a couple of international matches because I knew I just wasn't in the right frame of mind after a month of revising until two or three in the morning for my finals, and only a handful of training runs; but out in Malmo, in spite of its being cold, I found my strength suddenly flooding back, and expending physical energy instead of mental energy was very relaxing. I found I was full of running in the 800 metres, kicking with 200 metres to go and getting home with plenty to spare.'

═══════════

The Board member in charge was Doug Goodman, a large, bland, pleasant man with an unfortunate capacity for malapropisms on a grand scale. In Prague he had wished Brendan Foster good luck when he was lying on the massage table half an hour after he had competed. Now, late into the evening on the Sunday night in Malmo, he was engaged in an attempt to saddle the promoter of the Bislet Games in Oslo, Arne Haukvik, with half a dozen British make-weights. Seb was told he would not be cleared unless the Norwegians would pay expenses for the additional competitors, and it was not until two in the morning that Lynn Davies 'phoned Seb's room to tell him he was free to travel only hours later.

Bislet, nestling near the centre of the city and surrounded by high buildings which protect it from the wind, is an historic setting for countless world records. Over the years some forty have fallen, including many of the most notable. In 1955 Roger Moens of Belgium broke the German Rudolph Harbig's 800 metres record which, at 1:46·6, had resisted all assault for sixteen years. It was here in 1965, in the faint aroma of the nearby Frydenlund brewery, that Ron Clarke of Australia removed no less than 36 seconds from the 10,000 metres record. These, and many other records, had established a tradition which made Oslo the hunting ground of the great, urged on by a knowledgeable crowd who pressed close upon the six-lane track with its tight turns and worn synthetic surface. Yet the youthful Coe was peacefully unaware of most of this as he quietly checked in at the Panorama Somerhotell, high up on the fringe of the city beside the Sognsvatn Lake.

═══════════

❝I went out training on the Tuesday in the afternoon, after a loosening forty-minute run on the sandy paths around the lake when I first woke, and a series of warm-up 10 × 150 metres at midday. I was on my own, and after two 400 metres and a couple of 300 metres, I did a series of 200 metres in fractionally under 23. All this was an indication that I was in good shape. Grete Waitz (Norwegian holder of the women's marathon world record, and European 3,000 metres record) and her husband Jack had been watching, and without my knowing it Jack had also been timing me. He remarked with a smile that I was 'going well'. I felt that I should report the session, and back home Peter said 'go out and have a go. Run through the first lap in 50/50·5, then hang on and see what happens.' My own feeling was that if the wind died when the sun went down the next day I might get somewhere near the European record of 1:43·7. That night I went down into the town with John Walker and Rod Dixon, to an English cinema showing *California Suite*. Rod was all prepared for a late night out but Walker's wife was expecting a baby and he wanted to get back to the hotel, and I thought I could do with the sleep.❞

———————

Lennie Smith of Jamaica set a fast early pace, closely followed off the first bend by Coe and Mike Boit, but before they reached the 200 metres mark in under 25 it was obvious that something special was happening, because Boit and Evans White of America were already 20 metres adrift. Smith took Coe through the bell in 50·6, and now Coe was on his own, maintaining his rhythm all the way to the tape. Adrian Metcalfe, the commentator for ITV, almost lost his voice as he screamed, 'I don't believe it'. As Coe crossed the line he turned and saw Alan Pascoe, who looked shaken. 'What was it?' asked Coe, barely out of breath. 'Well, I've got 1:42 something' answered the astonished ex-hurdles champion. Walker had watched the race. 'The way he ran was just unbelievable. He looked

like he could run under 1:40, he never tied up at all. Seb
could win the 800 metres in Moscow and the 1,500 metres
in 1984, but he's got nothing to lose by going for both in
Moscow.' When Juantorena set a world record of 1:43·5
in Montreal it was supposed that he would dominate the
event for several years. But he only succeeded in remov-
ing another tenth from that time. In seventeen years the
1962 record set by Peter Snell had advanced less than a
full second. Now, on 5 July, Sebastian Coe astonished the
statisticians, and caused a ripple throughout athletics
around the globe, by lopping a complete second off Juantorena's time with an incredible 1:42·4, more than one and
a half seconds faster than he himself had run before.

———

❝ I had no particular sensation of speed and I think
I could have run even faster, I wasn't exhausted at all at
the end. I just followed the pace for the first lap which
after Prague, as it turned out, was exactly what Peter and
I had calculated the optimum would be. All I was thinking
to myself was, go on, get stuck in, start working. It was
easy. It was the 200 metres after the bell in 24·3 which
did it, that was where the record was born. I can remember
Dixon and Eamonn Coghlan and Brendan all shouting at
the beginning of the back straight. It was a strange feeling
– like being on auto-pilot; I was mentally outside what my
body was achieving, and it just felt beautiful. But I would
have been as happy on the night had I run 1:43·3 as I was
with 1:42·4. I found it difficult to adjust to the realization
that I was the holder of a world record. The feeling had
all been out there on the track. Now I changed out of my
running gear to leave the stadium with everyone else, and
found that I felt no different. I went and walked round the
track alone, to savour the place after the seventeen
thousand crowd had gone – and then found I had missed
the bus back to the hotel. When I tried to flag down one
or two cars going in the right direction they drove straight
by. Even Adrian Metcalfe (former Olympic quarter-miler
and now an ITV producer) went straight past without

noticing me. Eventually I managed to find a taxi and had what I suppose you might call my first ever real ego trip, when the driver refused the fare.**'**

=======

The entire British press was caught with its trousers down. Such was the modesty of the young man from Sheffield about his intentions in Oslo that none had followed him from Malmo and, with the approach of midnight, all were now left desperately trying to catch up with news from Reuters and the other foreign agencies. Soon the other leading two-lap men around the world were trying to adjust to the news. They would refuse to believe that Coe had not specifically prepared for the attempt, or that he had left the examination halls less than fit barely a month before. Rick Wohlhuter, the Montreal bronze medallist whose 1,000 metres Bislet-run record Coe would lower the following year, insisted: 'It had to be planned, nobody runs that sort of time without.' And former record holder Snell: 'I just hope he hasn't burned himself out a year too early.' Coe, meanwhile, was busy taking two planes, a ferry, and a two-and-a-half-hour car ride to honour a promise to run at a little mining town in northern Norway. He missed all the discussion and, instead, enjoyed himself on some mountain-stream salmon and a gentle 1:51.

=======

'I returned from Norway to a normal routine at home, working mainly on speed repetitions in preparation for the AAA Championships, where I'd planned to run the 400 metres. I travelled down to London for the meeting in a state of some alarm as a result of a highly indiscreet and totally unauthorized advertisement placed in *Athletics Weekly* by Mike Tagg of the Viga kit firm. It implied that, following my world record, I sanctioned their goods. Peter and I had to be quick to get hold of David Shaw, the new full-time general secretary of the Board who has done so much for relations between administra-

tion and athletes, to nip that problem smartly in the bud. I
ran 46·9 in the heats, easing up, then a personal best of
46·8 in the final, coming second to Kashif Hassan of
Sudan, who went on to win the World Cup. Then it was
back to Sheffield, up early on Sunday for a session of
repetitions along Rivelin Valley Road, and off to Oslo
again.**

The first Dubai Golden Mile, launched from the Middle
East and scheduled for Tokyo in September 1978, had
been cobbled together, largely in London by the West
Nally Organization who found the world's best milers
reluctant to travel to the Far East at the end of what had
already been a hard season. After much persuasion Ovett
went to give the event some of the lustre which would
otherwise have been absent, and won a slow tactical race,
with a kick over the last half lap, in 3:55·5. The American
Steve Scott finished a tired fourth behind Gonzales
(France) and young Graham Williamson. Only the first
three beat four minutes. Scott and his coach Len Miller
immediately planned revenge as their target for 1979 in
Oslo.

As a result of his invincible running over the previous
two seasons, Ovett's attitude in early 1979, publicly at
any rate, was that the best mile race in the world ought
to come to him at Crystal Palace following his victory in
Tokyo. A most laudable view if expressed in the interests
of British athletics. By degrees he talked himself into an
untenable position for what would turn out to be one of
the greatest races ever run. Having decided he could not
go to Oslo, he ventured that the race would be hollow
without him.

Scott was not the only one who aimed to 'peak' in Oslo.
Walker, the Olympic champion who had held the mile
record since the memorable first ever sub-3:50 run in
Gothenburg in 1975, was anxious to convince the public –
and himself – that he was still capable of great deeds. Fol-

lowing the Olympics he had suffered severely from inflamed tendons which had restricted his training, but in January 1979, running at Long Beach, California, he had set a new world indoor 1,500 metres best of 3:37·4. He would defend his mile record in Oslo with his blood. So highly prized did the invitations to this now truly golden mile become, that several notable athletes, among them Moorcroft, the Commonwealth champion, and the young Scot, John Robson, were kept waiting till close to the deadline. It was not until four days before the race that Robson clinched his place by finishing third in the AAA 1,500 metres. Coghlan, winning the AAA 5,000 metres in London with a personal best in a thrilling finish with Mike McLeod, and Dixon, the fastest miler of the year with his 3:52·9 in Philadelphia a month before, would be there.

Because NBC television had bought the rights to the race, it was essential to have an American interest in addition to Scott. So there were Craig Masback, a post-graduate student at Oxford, and Steve Lacy, who had run a 3:54·7 indoors and wanted to be in the race, but who, when most of the runners met at Haukvik's usual strawberry garden party, was reluctant to agree to the requests from Arne Haukvik and Andy Norman to make the pace. So was Williamson, another who had geared his season to this one race. Lacy said: 'I was in a difficult situation over making the pace; of course I wanted to be in the race, but I'd also had a bad throat for five days and considered I could only run to suit myself according to how I felt when I got out there.' Scott, denied his chance for revenge on Ovett, had planned for himself a more clearly defined objective:

'As much as wishing to win the race, I wanted to get that US record of Ryun's of 3:51·1; it was a definite psychological obstacle for me. I knew I was capable of it in the right race, and obviously the race had to be fast. I got together with Thomas Wessinghage, the European record holder, and, on the assumption that somebody would take us through the first half, agreed I'd push it out in the third lap and Tom would try and pick it up for the last quarter.'

Whatever the plans of these two, both Coghlan and Williamson reckoned the man to watch was Coe. So did
Walker. Seb himself was into new territory, and uncertain.
   Walker's opinion was: 'It's not the Golden Mile for
nothing. I've beaten all the athletes here many times. Coe
is the question mark, after his 800 metres. He's the
danger, nobody knows how good he can be. I just hope
that with 200 metres to go I'll be there kicking past him.'
Interviewed on television by NBC Coe had thought, 'it
calls for more specialized work than I've been doing'. This
would be only his fourth race over four laps in four seasons. He was the most inexperienced in the field and, on
paper, the third slowest. Only Bjorge Ruud, a Norwegian,
who would set the early pace, and Takashi Ishii of Japan
had not recorded a faster mile.

──────────

   ❬It was an awesome field, with the indoor and
outdoor world record holder, the European record holder,
the Commonwealth champion, and the second fastest
American of all time. Any of them could be the danger.
Walker was coming back, getting stronger, Scott was mentally hard, Coghlan had a big kick, but I reckoned Dave
Moorcroft might struggle because he was suffering from a
bad cold. Peter and I knew the third lap would be critical
for someone who was a jumped-up 800 metres runner and
not, on experience, a true miler. The record had never
entered our heads, to be quite honest I wasn't exactly sure
what it was! (I'm always terrible on statistics, and I had
made a real ass of myself on a TV sports quiz when I had
a mental blockage and couldn't remember who won the
1976 Olympic 1,500 metres.) Our aim was simply to win
the race. Something around 57 per lap is six seconds
slower than the record 800 metres pace, so it wasn't going
to feel too hard at first, but the guys with stamina were
going to be coming at me in that third lap. We discussed
the race over lunch; I thought it might be tactical but Peter
was convinced it would be fast, and said I should get close
to the front, stay there, and see how it worked out.❭

As father and son stood together after the warm up watching the event preceding the mile, the elder man said, 'you
can win this'. The younger said, 'I know'. He was feeling
good.

At the gun Coe jumped the other twelve runners to
avoid the mêlée on the first bend, but Lacy soon took
over, leading the runners into the back straight. He'd
decided to sacrifice himself as early pace setter because of
his weakened condition. Entering the second lap it was
Lacy from Scott and Wessinghage, with Coe fourth and
Coghlan and Walker bringing up the rear. Down the second back straight Moorcroft and Williamson were still in
contention. Lacy's first lap had been 57 exactly, Coe's
57·8. As they came into the home straight for the second
time there were still seven or eight of the thirteen in contention. Lacy reached the 880 yards in 1:54·5 and dropped out, and it was now that Scott, closely pursued by Coe
(1:55·3), jumped the pack. Into the fifth bend a clear gap
had opened with Wessinghage and Coghlan ten yards
adrift. Scott, with no sign of Wessinghage and no idea of
what was going on behind him, was obliged to drive harder
and earlier than he would have wished. It was his effort
over the next 300 yards, in the relentless pace of the third
lap, which now set up the record and finally killed off all
but Seb.

Into the home straight coming up to the bell Coe looked
perfectly relaxed, not a flicker of stress or emotion visible
in his face. Fifty yards from the bell he moved to Scott's
shoulder: for a moment the American thought it was Wessinghage making his contribution to the last quarter. With
a glance behind at the others, now fifteen yards down,
Coe made his move. His time at three laps was 2:53,
though he didn't hear it, which meant he had covered the
feared third quarter in 58. Now he needed fractionally
under 56 to break Walker's record. Walker, battling past
Coghlan into third place, heard the splits called to the
leaders and thought to himself 'it's gone'. Coe started the
last lap some three strides up on Scott, who was now the

only one near enough to offer a challenge. Walker, with a clear view of Coe's lead around the bend into the last back straight, would say later, 'I was preoccupied with watching him, knowing he was on the way to breaking my record'.

《The early pace did not disturb me, but all day I had been worrying about how I would feel on the third lap. I was prepared for it to hurt, but it didn't happen. It was not all that hard. With 600 yards to go I was wondering whether I should go to the front. At 500 yards I looked at the rest of the field and, apart from Scott, saw they were tiring. I was feeling very comfortable, so I stuck in hard for thirty or forty yards, got the gap over Scott, and then began to float.》

Around the last lap Coe pulled further away, never straining, while Scott's head went up in the vain effort to stay in touch. 'When Coe went, I should have gone too but I got isolated several yards back with nothing to "key" on, I just didn't know what he did was possible, but I guess it was no surprise to him or his father.' As Coe increased the lead to fifteen yards, passing the 1,500 metres in a European record of 3:32·8, the twenty thousand crowd was going wild with expectation, clapping rhythmically, those at the front hammering on the tin fence separating them from the track. Throughout the lap Coe was continually looking over his shoulder.

《I was afraid that someone would come surging up, I had a nagging doubt that I had done something wrong or unorthodox against a world class field, and that a big kicker would come through. When I looked back twice in the final straight it was fear not pain.》

Had he not slowed as he crossed the line, Seb's time would have been faster. Behind him, Scott agonizingly made the same error, eased over the last few yards and missed Ryun's twelve-year-old record by one hundredth of a second. Masback took third, Coghlan fourth, and Robson pipped Walker by half a stride for fifth. Williamson, who, but for losing a shoe on the final bend might have got third, was seventh in 3:53·2, two and a half seconds inside Paunonen's European junior record. In this incredible race the first ten all finished under 3:55·3. As Coe crossed the line there was pandemonium. Peter had sprinted across from the back straight. 'Have I?' asked Seb. 'Yes' said his father, who would add reprovingly later: 'The lesson of the Golden Mile was the one which the first two to finish ignored: run through the tape!'

❢ I was astonished when Peter said it was a world record, I had no idea it had been that fast. I went on a lap of honour, someone pushed a Union Jack in my hands on the back straight. It was tied to a pole upside down, but that didn't matter just then! It was marvellous to have brought the record back to Britain after twenty-two years, when it was held by another Yorkshireman. ❡

A trail of photographers followed him around the track and Masback, a familiar figure on the British scene who had surprised everyone with his own tremendous finish, observed: 'Seb looked like a combination of the Pied-Piper of Hamelin and Delacroix's *Liberty Leading the People*.' As the Scandinavian summer faded into that beautiful mellow half-light which lasts till next sunrise, the athletes made their way in ones and twos to the customary reception and dinner. Neil Allen of the London *Evening Standard*, for many years perceptive athletics correspondent of *The Times*, reported next morning:

> 'At ten thirty last night, in the restaurant of an Oslo
> sports club, Sebastian Coe felt the first inkling of what it
> is like to be regarded as a giant of modern sport. He
> and his father had arrived late after telephoning Mrs
> Coe in Sheffield to talk about her son's stunning world
> record. As the Coes stepped into the room, a treasure
> trove of Olympic gold medallists and world record
> holders – men like Ed Moses, Don Quarrie, Miklos
> Nemeth, John Walker, Rod Dixon, and Brendan Foster
> – stood and burst into applause. Sebastian stood there
> looking embarrassed, and then gave a little nod of
> thanks before busying himself at the self-service
> counter. Our new record holder is capable of under
> 3:47, but future times matter little to me today, remem-
> bering the incredible sight of Coe running further and
> further away from the his almost mesmerized rivals,
> until he took his last faltering step.'

As the US *Track and Field News* reported: 'What stunned
most observers was his almost complete lack of fatigue
after the race. No stumbling, no heavy breathing.'

———————

    ‘I felt sorry for John Walker, he was obviously
very depressed. Everyone who wanted a photo of me
wanted him with me. Even though he'd said he wanted to
be in the race when his record went, I didn't envy him, I
knew how I'd feel when it happened to me – even though
from the start I tried to take the attitude that my records
were merely temporary and borrowed. John reacted with
great dignity when he received press calls from New Zealand immediately after the race, and said that it was a
great occasion and that he was pleased for me. For a
while, as with the 800 metres, I found it difficult to grasp
what I had done. I was overwhelmed by the compliment
which all those other great athletes, including John, had
paid me in the restaurant. It really hit me, I suppose, on

the 'plane going home when an air hostess came up to me just before we landed in Manchester and asked if I would leave first. When I got out on top of the steps there were about forty photographers on the tarmac, and I thought, wow! I was ushered through customs without having to show my passport. Malcolm Brammer, the sports editor from Radio Sheffield and an old friend, and Peter Cooper of the *Daily Mirror*, had driven over to meet us. They took us home and we found the road was jammed from end to end, with two film crews in the front garden vying for the first interview, and a whole load of photographers who had apparently been there for up to five hours. Eventually I got inside, and for the next few days the family spent most of the time saying I wasn't there – which was true. I was out training to get into shape for Turin and Zürich. **9**

<hr>

At the Europa Cup Final in Turin East Germany carried off both the men's and women's trophies for the third successive occasion. The outstanding individual was Harald Schmid of West Germany with an exceptional double, inside an hour, in the 400 metres hurdles and flat. On the second day Allan Wells silenced the 35,000 crowd in the Stadio Communale with the first defeat of Pietro Mennea by a European over 200 metres for six years, a result which Mennea would reverse in Moscow. The line up for the 800 metres included both Wulbeck of painful Helsinki memory, and Beyer, the thief of Prague, and so gave Seb the scope for a double revenge of sorts.

<hr>

6 I could see the headlines if I failed. I'd never before been *expected* to win anything. The prospects frightened me a bit, the realization that for the first time I was running under pressure not for myself but for the team. I wasn't helped by one or two team officials coming up to me and saying that because I was three seconds faster on

paper, all I had to do was go out and run from the front –
just as if it was a question of driving down to the garage
to fill up the car. Peter and I hadn't talked for two weeks.
He was away on holiday, but what we had agreed was that
it was *unnecessary* to run from the front. Apart from anything else, I was sick to death of so many people during
the past year or more saying that I could *only* run from
the front and that I could not run without Peter's being
there. Even coaches need holidays! I travelled down to the
stadium with Brendan and we passed some German
supporters chanting, 'Bey-er, Bey-er'. Brendan simply said,
'forget it, go out there and bloody win something for the
first time in your life'. It was a friendly, calculated insult,
and it was true that the only championship I'd won was
the indoor at San Sebastian.

Warming up before the start I refused to look at Wulbeck when he tried to shake hands; I knew that if I
accepted his apology for what happened two years previously I would have conceded an advantage. I ran a really
cagey race, and was last at the bell. It unnerved those at
the front, they were glancing back for me. I moved up to
fourth with 200 metres to go, and put in a sprint of 24·4
to finish in front of Zivotic of Yugoslavia with plenty to
spare. Wulbeck was third and Beyer fifth. Although the
time of 1:47·3 was almost five seconds outside the record,
the race did a lot for my confidence. As I ran towards the
line I raised my arms in relief, but when I saw it on video
afterwards it made me cringe, and I determined not to do
that again. In the dope-test room I made up a fruit drink
from the dispenser for Wulbeck and myself, and we shook
hands.❜

The press reluctantly returned home from Turin, where
Jim Coote's seat in the stadium had remained poignantly
empty and a spray of orchids had been put on his desk
from the Italian sports writers' association. They left
behind the enviable tranquillity of the press club – presented by Fiat millionaire Agnelli – with its tennis courts

and restaurants and vast swimming-pool, around which in summer are draped some of the city's most elegant ladies, whose husbands pay up to one thousand pounds per annum in order that they may be seen escorting some of the best tans in Italy.

Seb went off to Viareggio for a small-town meeting where he has run for some years – not least because of the all-night Italian knees-up which follows the racing! After this recreational, end-of-season pit-stop, he moved to the Swiss mountain sports training centre at Macolin, high above Lake Neuchâtel. There, he was able to fill his lungs with the pure mountain air and the aroma of pine needles, running free as a deer among the forest paths skirting verdant meadows, with their ample, bell-ringing cows. There is a peacefulness up at Macolin which, in conjunction with first rate physiotherapy and that special brand of comfy, hygienic Swiss hospitality, makes it a haven for sportsmen. Meanwhile, down in Zürich Andreas Brugge, wealthy promoter of the annual Weltklasse meeting, was busy resisting Ovett's requests to be asked to run in his 1,500 metres. Ovett was told, through Andy Norman, that he could have the 800 metres. Brugge's thinking was that Ovett's inclusion in the 1,500 metres would make it a tactical race and, without having said as much to the Coes, he was looking for another world record from Seb to enhance the stature of a meeting which has been growing yearly. Calculated leaks to the Swiss press meant that by the time Seb arrived down in the crowded, carnival mood of the Nova Park Hotel, it had been established in the public mind that he *was* going for a third record.

――――――――

⁶ In particular, an interview with Swiss TV put the pressure on me; the record wasn't something I'd been sitting thinking about up at Macolin. I'd agreed to run in Zürich the previous March. But when the rest of the world *thinks* you've said you will go for it, you're overtaken by events outside your control. Peter arrived from holiday in the Adriatic the same night as me, and told me

he'd thought out the lap times for a record *if* the weather
was right. We both knew there was a chance for three-
in-a-row, which might never come again, but it depended
on the weather because we reckoned that I was not going
to get too much help from the field. **'**

It was a warm day but close, and as the evening came on
a swirling wind got up and an angry sky closed in from the
surrounding Alps. As Peter and Seb sat having a coffee
following his afternoon sleep, there was the sound of distant thunder; they looked at each other and doubted that
it was 'on'. As they walked out of the Nova Park at
around 9.00 p.m. to stroll the quarter of a mile to the
grass warm-up area, the dust off the pavement kicked up
in their faces and, with the increase in wind, it was getting
colder. Inside the stadium, Wells had been battling it out
with James Sanford (US) and James Gilkes (Guyana) for
the Dubai Sprint Championship, running into a two metres
per second wind. Wells took the silver medal on aggregate
over the two races. From high in the press box we could
see the indigo clouds and the lightning illuminating the
city. But as the runners came to the line, Seb looking
more tense and nervous than in either of the Oslo races,
the wind indulgently slackened and the flags on the
stadium roof drooped on their poles. Kip Koskei of Kenya
went off at a spendthrift pace, immediately imperilling any
record, for a first lap in 54·2, with Seb obliged to hold
on a yard or so down in a suicidally fast 54·4.

'I was very much aware of the crowd and their
obvious expectation. Koskei set off at what I knew
instantly was too fast a pace, and at the end of the first
lap Peter was bellowing at me to slow down. He didn't
need to tell me, and we covered the next 400 metres in 59
and were now nearly twenty metres up on Mike Boit. I'd

already agreed with Peter before the start, when he'd said, 'it's shit or bust, get out there and hang on'. We'd thought the field might get me through two and a half laps, but with 750 metres still to go I realized I was no longer getting any help from Koskei, so I just had to move in front. I remember suddenly seeing the track empty in front of me as I went by, and knowing there were still almost two whole laps remaining. With an 800 metres time of 1:53, which Peter had yelled at me coming off the fourth bend, I knew the record was there if I wanted it badly enough. I can still today hear the roar from the Swiss crowd as I went in front, and it was that which lifted me.'

Seb went through that third lap in a brave 57·6, passing the bell in 2:35·3 and the 1,200 metres in 2:50·8. He had needed 56·9 over the last lap and he did it in 56·8, shaving a tenth of a second off Filbert Bayi's glorious Christchurch run in the 1974 Commonwealth Games with 3:32·03. In forty-one days he had run himself into athletic immortality. No man in history had ever held all three records simultaneously – the 800 metres, the mile, and now the metric mile. Giants of the past, such as Glenn Cunningham, Sydney Wooderson, Jim Ryun, Gunder Hägg, and Peter Snell had held two of the three but never the lot, though Ryun had held the 880 yards in 1:44·9 at the same time as the mile and 1,500 metres in 1967. Coe was the first Briton to hold the 1,500 metres since official International Amateur Athletics Federation records began in 1913, and how the crowd had responded to the lone, frail figure in the British vest as he ran on and on.

'I will never forget that draining run to the finish, the crowd were tremendous with their encouragement, and it's the race of which I am proudest in terms of endurance. If I'd had the pacing for longer I'm sure I

could have run under 3:30. But immediately it was over I
just wanted to get away from the track, anywhere. Physically it had been hard, but the mental exhaustion was
total, and when I got back to the hotel room with Peter
there was a feeling of colossal anti-climax, an emptiness,
and I had no feeling of enjoyment or excitement. I would
never want to go through that particular race again. It is
difficult to describe the effort it cost me afterwards to go
out and do an interview with the BBC, I was in a daze.

Peter flew back to Italy and I stayed a few days in London getting ready for the Rotary Games. I was out training in Richmond Park, being paced by a friend in a car,
when we were stopped by the park police and accused of
causing obstruction for going too slowly! By the time we
had had an argument over something I thought seemed a
bit unreasonable I'd cooled down, and pulled a calf muscle
when I started up again, so I missed the Rotary. I went to
the meeting and was given a marvellous reception by the
crowd which really meant a great deal to me. From the
press box I watched Steve have a go at the mile record,
but although Peter Browne took him through the half-way
on schedule, the third lap lagged. Graham Williamson,
who had arrived straight from an eighteen-hour flight from
Mexico, where he had won the World Student Games
1,500 metres, just couldn't push out the third lap, even
though Steve was yelling 'faster!' in his ear. It was Steve's
thirteenth race in five weeks, five of them abroad, and he
was simply tired.

When I got home the family was still away. There were
so many letters on the door-mat that I could hardly open
the front door. My mother and George and I were still
answering them in November, and were grateful when the
International Athletes Club offered to pay for secretarial
assistance.'

<hr />

Among the letters was one from Czechoslovakia addressed
simply: 'Sebastian Coe, Great Britain'. Life for the boy
from Sheffield was never going to be quite the same again.

(Syndication International Ltd)

The breakthrough. Seb wins the 1977 Emsley Carr Mile at Crystal Palace from 1,500m world record holder, Filbert Bayi, in 3:57.7

'I hope this is hurting him more than it hurts me!' Loughborough bio-mechanics expert, George Gandy, stretches a hamstring

(Bela Domokos)

(*Bela Domokos*)

Relaxing and limbering up along the sandy, pine-needle-strewn paths around the tranquil Sognsvaten Lake behind Oslo's Sommerhotell, prior to the Golden Mile world record in 1979

(*Bela Domoko*

(*Bela Domokos*)

'Someone gave me a Union Jack, it was upside down, but what did that matter!' Britain's Golden Miler

Leading Steve Scott of America into the penultimate bend at Bislett, having just gone to the front in the Golden mile, setting a world record of 3:49.0

(*The Associated Press Ltd*)

All alone at the finish of the 1,500m in Zurich, with a world record of 3:32.1

'At fourteen I knew he was good, at sixteen I had a strange kind of certainty that if I was patient I had a world beater.' Happiness, pride, and satisfaction for father and son

(Bela Domokos)

'Where do I go from here?' Help from a friendly Telford policeman shortly after Seb's three world records

(Bela Domokos)

ela Domokos)

'Now for Moscow!' With Peter after the 1,000m world record at Bislett in 1980

Receiving the 1979 BBC Sportsview Personality of the Year Award from
Sir Roger Bannister, the first man to break four minutes for the mile (above)

Posing by the plaque commemorating Bannister's historic run (top right)

Loughborough University team photo, 1980. Seb is flanked by Wendy Smith and
Chris Boxer (centre right)

Studying form with Angela and Nick before the Ivo Van Damme Memorial meeting in
Brussels (below right)

On this track on May 6th 1954
ROGER GILBERT BANNISTER
Exeter College
President O.U.A.C. 1948–1949
ran one mile
in 3 minutes 59·4 seconds
Thus becoming the first man to run
one mile in less than four minutes.

(Oxford Mail)

(Syndication International Ltd)

(Bela Domokos)

(Bela Domokos)

Lucky the East Germans didn't see this one! Seb, whose wonder drug is tea at Borough Road, lines up for the 1,500m in the 1980 meeting at Isleworth. (Sean Butler wears number 8)

(Bela Domokos)

A fifth 'world record': the fastest ever 800m on a cinder track (1:44.9) in the 1980 Loughborough v AAA match at Loughborough

His one regret of the season was that after the Oslo Golden Mile he had been sent by Sir Roger Bannister the last of a special issue of ties for sub-four-minute milers and he forgot to wear it when receiving the BBC Sportsview Personality of the Year award in London from Sir Roger.

5 : Countdown

‘During my many discussions with Brendan Foster, he has mentioned from time to time the pressure of
well-wishers, weighing down upon him during the eight
months or so before the Olympic Games in Montreal. The
fact that he couldn't go out to the supermarket with his
wife in Newcastle, for instance, without the sixtieth person
that day coming up to him and slapping him on the back
and saying, 'you're going to bring back the gold medals,
aren't you?' Now, in the autumn of 1979, exactly the
same was happening to me in Sheffield. I'd have people
shouting at me over fences, on passing buses, from half-
way up telegraph poles, and out of holes in the ground,
not to mention all those in every shop I visited. I went to
Hepworth's for my official British suit, and the whole shop
stopped work. I must have had seventeen people measur-
ing me all at once, and the look of expectation on their
faces, and the knowledge that I would be carrying all that
with me, and from thousands like them, obviously became
a burden. Usually, nothing really bothers me. I suppose I
am toughening up a little, and for much of the time that
autumn the Olympics might just as well have been July
1981. I've never really felt the pressure of *time*. In the
past, when Peter has been wanting to sit down a week or
even ten days before a race to work out tactics, I've said
'OK, OK, later'. There's something inside me which never

82

wants to switch on until it's absolutely necessary. I didn't feel particularly under pressure from my records, though I was aware of them. The pressure came from people around me, outside the family, behaving unnaturally, constantly worrying about my health where they had never bothered in the past. 'Oh no, not a cold!' or, 'How's the leg?', or, *Do* sit in the back' – from people who you *know* have never before worried about their passenger's seat belt. With that lot, of course, you're not sure whether they are worrying too much or whether they just don't know what to say.

But there is the other lot who are convinced that you must be wanting to go on the razzle every evening, and that *their* working life is infinitely harder than *yours*. They tend to think that just because you're a student at Loughborough you lead a privileged life. They don't realize, and I suppose there is no reason why they should, that you have to get up to go training before lectures and go training again afterwards. I've been out to dinners where everyone is so well meaning that things have dragged on till past 1.00 a.m. when I've wanted to be away by 11.30 p.m. And when I've excused myself – saying I've got to be on the road by 8.00 a.m. – they've looked slightly offended, and have said they've had to be at the factory or market by 7.00 a.m., as if physically it was the same thing. There are always one or two who come up and offer you a cigar, as if they suppose that what you're doing is not *really* all that different from what they are doing. Not that I'm complaining, because many people are very kind, it's just that they don't realize the asceticism of the life one is obliged to lead. I might like a brandy, or even a cigar, but that's something which will have to wait. And there are some who are just plain bloody blunt, and say to you as if they were being *so* amusing, 'well, if you don't come back with any medals nobody will want to know you'.

There is a tremendous tendency for the public to take you over. In the autumn, after the records, I was due to go over to Telford, only socially, to a grass-track meeting. It was the first time I really realized just what sort of position I was now in. Frank Bough mentioned the event on television, and when I arrived there were 15,000 people or more at a place which wasn't equipped to cope with 5,000. I don't think there were more than a couple of policemen. I'd agreed to autograph some postcard photos, but people started tearing down the tent where I was sitting from all sides, and George Gandy only managed to avoid a nasty situation by announcing that if people sent their names and addresses to Loughborough, we would guarantee to send the cards. That cost us a pound or two in postage! Not to mention the time. To cap it all, Bough had signed off the TV programme by saying, without thinking, 'what an *attractive* young man'. I got the most impossible stick for months afterwards. I couldn't go anywhere without ribald remarks being made. If only people on television realized what one line can do to you. Television is a marvellous medium for reporting the news, for documentaries, and the arts, but it takes gross liberties in its treatment of people's private lives, which is why my family rejected a request to co-operate on *This is Your Life*.

I'd be lying if I said I didn't enjoy a lot of television, watching my favourite club Chelsea play when I cannot get there myself, and it's nice to be able to see my own races on video to check exactly what happened in front of me if I lost, or behind me if I won. I was gratified when I won the 1979 Sportsview award, but there is a tendency for television people to suppose that you *must* be grateful and willing to co-operate in anything *they* decide they want to do.

I've got some good friends in Yorkshire TV, but someone really went over the top after the world records in 1979. A secretary 'phoned to say I was going to be Sportsman of the Year, and would I be there in Leeds in January for the programme. I said I couldn't be as I was going to be out of the country. It was eventually agreed, after persistent messages from the producer Laurie Higgins, that I would go to the Leeds studios before Christmas instead to record an interview, and I arranged a whole weekend around the date. I received a third-hand message at thirty-six hours' notice to say it was off because of a technicians' strike. We next received a message from Higgins saying that it was imperative that I should do the programme after Christmas. I said I was sorry about the union problem, but I had my own problems and could not be there. The next thing we knew there was a film unit in the front garden demanding an interview in our sitting-room. It was a few days before Christmas and we had a house full! Peter told the chap in charge, 'I don't think you've got the message', but he replied, shoving his foot in the door, 'this is going to rebound badly on you'. They left without their interview, and we next had Higgins on the 'phone saying, 'well, if Sebastian can't go to Leeds, what's his coach doing? Who is his coach?' It was all very unfortunate, and the upshot was that the YTV Sportsman of the Year for 1979 was Kevin Keegan!

Although I was still working at Loughborough on a post-graduate degree, I could spread the academic load over two years at my own discretion. In the autumn of 1979, partly because of the social functions which in most instances I found it very difficult to refuse, I spent more time at home. It brought me a lot closer to my younger brother Nick, enabling him to feel that I was really part of the family, not just someone who came home occasionally, took what I wanted and went away again. We had an hour's tennis now and then: I hadn't had a solid hour with Nick in four years and his irrepressible humour was invaluable in the months leading up to the Olympics. I was able to go to a good provincial theatre again, and to see the inside of the Graves Art Gallery in Sheffield. Ironically, with more time on my hands, I watched a lot less television. At Loughborough, because I was always tired after training, I would just slump in front of the telly, which is an atrocious waste of time.

During the last couple of months of 1979 I could easily have eaten three dinners a night – providing I had been prepared to give three speeches. Again, I'm not complaining. I loved my success on the track and the prestige which it brought, the goodwill towards me from complete strangers. But it was clear I would have to get out of the country if I was going to spend the winter preparing pro-

perly for the Olympics. Not only would that prevent me
from being drowned in goodwill, but I would be able to
find somewhere away from the inhibiting cold of northern
England. It wasn't that I wanted to be a recluse, just that
I needed two or three months of concentrated, uninter-
rupted training away from the public eye.

With the help of a close friend, Peter and I were able to
arrange something that was perfect. From the New Year
until March I was able, perhaps for the one and only time
in my life, to be a full-time athlete. I'd always been
interested in how Steve could train in the morning and
then go back to bed until midday, get up and do another
run, sleep all afternoon, wake up for another session in
the evening, have a meal, and go back to bed. I tried this
sort of schedule for a day when I was in Oslo before the
mile. Up early, run round the lake, breakfast, back to bed,
some striding, sleep after lunch, an evening session on the
track at Bislet, back to the hotel for a meal and bed by
9.30 p.m. For one day I was a full-time athlete. I don't
want to deride that kind of preparation. It may suit Steve,
but temperamentally it didn't suit me. Yet Peter and I
knew that to withstand the very special demands of the
Olympics, with six or possibly seven races in the space of
nine days, I *had* to have a winter working full-time for
at least a few months to be able to match other great runners who would be preparing with the same thoroughness.
I did it once, yet I doubt if I would ever do it again.'

———

Twenty miles or so to the north-west of Rome on the way
to Viterbo, along the winding, fir-lined Via Cassia, just
beyond the grand-prix circuit which the Romans call a
ring-road, is the sprawling village of Olgiata. The roadside
is bordered by the usual cafés and petrol stations, and here
and there smart new apartment blocks with expensive
landscaped gardens entered by self-locking gates. A couple
of hundred yards off the road is one of those large,
guarded estates, where the well-heeled, and occasionally
the famous, the diplomatic, or the Middle East super-rich

come to reside in sanctuary and security, and – equally important – in anonymity, away from the frenetic city. Behind high wire fences are ten square miles of woodland, a rolling golf course, and, behind exotic shrubbery, the sort of air-conditioned houses with large picture windows which in England would require a substantial five-figure salary to maintain, let alone to buy. The two entrances are attended night and day, East-European style, by armed guards whose lethargic attitude somewhat belies their instructions to ensure that the unfriendly and unwanted do not gain admittance. There are twenty miles or so of reasonably well maintained private road, the golf course has fairways as wide as St Peter's Square, laid out more with leisure in mind than competition. The club house boasts that kind of casual elegance for which the Italians have no peer – thick carpets on polished wood floors, huge enveloping armchairs and Chesterfields, a bridge room, and a white-blazered bar-man whose bar never closes. In mid-morning you are as likely to see Sophia Loren's mother taking coffee, as an automobile millionaire in Daks plus-fours taking a rather stiff swing on the first tee. The first requirement of membership, apart from your bank balance – which is more stringently selective than any committee – is discretion and good manners. Thus it was that Sebastian Coe was accepted, quietly and almost without notice, throughout the winter of 1979 as he laid the foundations for one of the most rigorous races he would ever run.

Here he passed a hundred days in soothing, gentle sunshine, his limbs cushioned on the rolling grassland or the forest circuit, at times sharing them with gleaming thoroughbreds, their four legs not all that substantially swifter than his two. The only residents who marred his stay were the prowling, aggressive dogs, kept roaming free in their gardens by many of the householders. Fortunately for Seb, the friend's house where he stayed contained only a couple of white cats. There he could be found some lunchtimes, quietly doing the hoovering while the owners were away. He had his jazz tapes, a selection of books, and the flexibility to train not just when he needed to but,

more valuably, when he was in the mood. There were
days when he felt he would never lose another race. The
training was perfectly balanced between sessions of lifting
anything up to an accumulative total of twelve tons, in
weight training at the English school a mile or two down
the public road beyond the compound, and the soaring,
scorching runs of six or ten miles which would carry him
across the golf course almost as fast as a seven iron could
drive a ball.

‹ The choice of destination, knowing that I had to
get away from England, was pretty narrow in the end.
There was the New Zealand–Australian summer circuit or
the US indoor circuit, but I didn't want to race, and nor
did I want to spend the time talking shop with other athletes. I could have gone to the Finnish training school in
southern Spain, but that would have been too public, and
I didn't want to stay in a hotel. So it was fortunate that we
had friends, whom we had known long before they left
England, in Rome. I was able to afford it, travelling to
and from home and paying my way out there, thanks to
my sponsorship from the Sports Aid Foundation and Otis.
But the greatest value of all of the place, privacy apart,
was the intensity, regularity, and quality of .the training.
I'd run three world records after a low-key winter of
appalling conditions and a handful of high-pressure weeks
after my exams finished in June. But in Olgiata, for the
first time in my life, I was able to organize myself, physically, as I wanted to. I suppose you could say, if it doesn't
sound too much like boasting, that I'd run the records on
natural talent. Out in Italy I was able to lay the foundations of something much more lasting and permanent.
Admittedly, there were some evenings when I couldn't lift
my head out of the chair to go upstairs to bed and be
ready for the next day's onslaught. But I did see a bit of
Rome: some beautiful opera and some very dull Italian
league soccer. I did on one occasion slip down to the
Olympic Stadium for a bit of a work out, and it was lovely

to be back on a track again. There was the temptation to
let rip, but that could have been damaging and might have
attracted the attention of some passing journalists, so I
just played it cool, did some striding, and then disap-
peared back down the Via Cassia. Certainly I was tired a
lot of the time, but there is so much more value in training without mental stress from the hassle of other
activities. And when I wasn't tired, I was able to start
reading for pleasure again for the first time in years.'

At intervals Peter flew to Rome to monitor the training
and the progress of *his* thoroughbred.

'The records didn't really affect our preparation for the
Olympics. What they had given us was confirmation that
our methods were right, plus the knowledge that Seb
had more natural talent than we had supposed. What
we needed now in training was the same, only more so.
For the first time we could enter a track season with a
whole winter of unbroken preparation. The only slight
difference out at Olgiata was a concentration on
stamina, because of the packed Olympic schedule. The
build-up on speed would come on the early season
track, mainly with a series of 800 metres. By the time
he came back to England, Seb would have to meet a
series of targets in training sessions on the track.'

On Easter Monday, his friends having returned home to
England on holiday, Seb carefully put away the crockery
in the kitchen, packed his tapes and his running shoes and,
after a vain search for the cats, said good-bye to his oasis
of the last three months. As we turned the corner at the
top of the road, heading down towards the main gate of
the compound, we observed that the cats, too, had gone
away for the week-end, and were enjoying the sun in a
neighbour's garden; they had their own back door entrance. The next hour or so was something like Rimsky-
Korskakov's 'Flight of the Bumblebee' as we buzzed our
way round the ring-road, overtaken and overtaking on

both sides, to pick up the Autostrada del Sol to Florence
and Milan, where Seb was due to run in a specially organ-
ized road race at the little shoe-manufacturing town of
Vigevano. Once on the freeway, where we discovered the
toll-keepers were all taking the day off, it was a glorious
run through undulating Tuscany under a forget-me-not-
blue sky. Pausing for a cup of tea at a service centre outside Bologna, we were offered the usual cut-price trousers
and fur coats by unshaven Yugoslavians. Losing our way
south of Milan when leaving the autostrada, we arrived
late in the evening to find Peter *agitato*.

I wasn't sure who looked the more fretful, him or the
Italian organizers of the race, having had visions, no
doubt, of their would-be champion somewhere in a ditch
beside the road. Seb had, in fact, telephoned to advise his
hosts that he might be late, and quietly took his father on
one side to release some of the steam before a gasket was
blown. The next problem to be overcome was the fact that
the race had been routed through and round this beautiful
fifteenth-century town, with its inspiring Leonardo da
Vinci main square, so that most of it was over cobble-
stones! Three months' work could be undone in a quarter
of an hour. Peter and Seb, having inspected the course by
moonlight, stated that if it could not be altered he could
not run. With the entire population, down to the newest
babe in arms, scheduled to turn out to watch in a little
over twelve hours' time, with the bunting already marking
the course, which would be specially closed to all traffic,
and with the mayor and the chief of police already in bed,
and unlikely to rise early enough to sanction a last minute
change, the organizers looked as if they might burst into
tears. However, the nation renowned for its resourceful-
ness in fixing things duly did so, and on a lovely day Seb
coasted clear of a field that included international road
runners, to enter the square at the finish like some Sir
Galahad, to a huge ovation. Even the *carabinieri* clapped.
Hardly breathing after five miles in under twenty-five
minutes, Seb put on his tracksuit and went looking for
some shampoo before meeting the mayor for lunch.

Back home in Yorkshire he had an appointment of con-

siderable significance with physiologist Professor John
Humphreys at Leeds Polytechnic, where he was to be
subjected to every imaginable test in order to measure
the effect of his winter's work. They stuck a long rubber
tube in his mouth, sellotaped electrodes to all his arterial
signal boxes, put him on a tread-mill, and told him to start
running – in order to measure the efficiency of oxygen
uptake and pulse-rate in relation to pace.

‹ After twenty to twenty-five minutes the machine
was beginning to smoke and so was I! Neither of us could
go any faster, and I was doing around twenty miles an
hour. Put simply, the results told me that my winter's
work had been more valuable than ever before. ›

Humphreys, who felt obliged by the results to check
his apparatus, was able to reveal that Seb now had an
oxygen efficiency equivalent to the top marathon runners,
and suggested that whereas normal athletes had one gear
and outstanding athletes two gears, Seb, physiologically,
had three. Armed with this knowledge, with the evidence
of the previous year's records, and the logical projection of
his latest training onto performance on the track, Seb sat
back with me one afternoon to make an objective assessment of his Olympic prospects in his two distances. His
calm, almost detached conclusions, as realistic as an
astronaut accepting without question that NASA has got
its sums right, were frighteningly emphatic.

‹ In the 800 metres I don't think there is really a
serious challenge. No one. James Maina of Kenya might
be a medallist if the Kenyans go. He is 1·5 seconds slower
on paper, which may not be much physically but, at that
sort of pace, it's considerable physiologically. If the race is

fast, there will be nobody else who knows what it's like under 1:43. I've been there before, and I know it doesn't hurt, and that I'm in better shape than last year. I think there are one or two who will give Steve some bother in the 800 metres if it's fast. In the 1,500 metres it *should* be between Steve and me. I think Masback and Scott (if the Americans go), and Coghlan and Straub will be in for third place.'

We were sitting in my garden. Seb had allowed himself the rare treat of a Campari as we idly watched George the tortoise making tracks for his favourite resting place, between runs, among the roots of a fir tree. Although I had become accustomed over several years to Seb's realistic assessment of any situation, this forecast, which I agreed with basically, took my breath away when stated so baldly. To be that *certain* in your own mind was to carry around a responsibility to yourself which could be unnerving.

'It is possible to psyche yourself up for something without really believing it deep down. But if you genuinely do believe it, there's no hiding from it. It's like breaking a stick of rock and finding the writing's the same all the way through. It's a far worse situation to be in, knowing that you have to do something stupid *not* to win a race, than thinking that you will have to do something startling if you *are* to win it. There was nothing, including Steve, that I'd seen at either distance which worried me.'

I immediately began to conceive of him winning the 800 metres, running from the front in the most dramatic fashion like Bayi in the Commonwealth 1,500 metres. What about it? The idea appealed to him, but he and Peter had already discussed tactics, with two months still to go, and

had arrived at a basic plan, more or less similar for both
races: that he would sit in on the leaders, never allowing
himself to get out of touch, and strike, Ovett-style, in the
last 150–250 metres, on the basis that, whatever the pace
of either race up to that point, he could not be 'dropped';
and that whatever the remaining portion of the race, he
could cover it faster than anyone else still in contention. It
was a fail-safe approach, used so devastatingly by Ovett in
over forty consecutive races. But how would he cope with
the temperamental shock of coming away with defeat in
one, or both, races?

⸻

᠎ ❬ It would be a disappointment, but it would only
last until the next time I had to go out for a racing performance. That is not to say that I do not desperately
want to do well. I do. I want to succeed very much, simply
for the work I've put in, and which Peter has put in, and
for the effort of the family. But if it doesn't come off I
won't walk through the rest of my life a failure. I would
know I had failed at that time, but I could accept honest
failure – being beaten on the day by someone who had
proved himself the better man. That is the name of the
game. I remember listening to the radio on the morning of
the 1974 F.A. Cup Final, and hearing Alec Stock, the
Fulham manager, saying: 'Some players will wake up feeling it's just another day, others that they will end the day
with blood in their boots.' That's how I hope it will be
with me. That if I fail, I will do so having given my best. ❭

⸻

In the light of events, they were to prove poignant words.
At that stage it was by no means certain that Britain
would be going to the Olympics. The government, led by
Mrs Thatcher, was making repeated requests to individual
athletes and to the British Olympic Association chairman,
Sir Denis Follows, to stage a voluntary boycott of the
Games, in line with American policy as laid down by Presi-

dent Carter – and reluctantly accepted by US sportsmen
and women. While the argument raged, and the elderly
but adamant Follows was twice summoned to Downing
Street without yielding, Seb adroitly sat on the fence. This
was not indecision. He understood the dilemma perfectly,
and had not yet made up his own mind. I had by then
given my personal opinion in the columns of the *Daily
Express*: Britain was wrong to send teams either to South
Africa – the Lions rugby team – or to Moscow. I well
knew, after extensive travelling over twenty years in every
Eastern European country including Albania, the extent of
the erosion there of personal liberties which every man
and woman in Britain takes for granted. I had friends
behind the Iron Curtain whose experiences were appalling,
but I was careful not to attempt to put any pressure on
Seb, whose position was utterly different from mine. Privately, I felt it would be a noble gesture if he withdrew,
knowing his confidence in his success, but it was in no way
my position to influence him. Regarding my own *practical*
involvement, I considered that, as in war, the journalist
must suspend his own moral views in the matter, and go
and report the facts. Having gone, the facts merely streng-
thened my existing views on the inhumanity of the Russian régime, but they altered my view on the boycott.

   With hindsight, I believe that the West should have
flooded Russia with as many visitors as possible, to make
as much contact as possible with ordinary Soviet people in
order to strengthen their resolve in their quest for the
freedom of thought and speech and work and travel which
they are denied. Seb was in a much more difficult position
as a prominent international sportsman, knowing that the
premature public expression of any decision he made
would be used as an implement of persuasion by those
whose view he supported. He did not wish to be the
public Litmus paper. Even so, some innocuous remarks
made to Alan Hubbard, the sports correspondent of *Now*
magazine, were picked up by the Russian Tass news
agency, twisted, and distorted into a personal attack on
Mrs Thatcher. They were reproduced by, of all papers, the
Daily Telegraph. It was doubly irritating, because he had

leaned over backwards to retain a neutral public front. As
an intelligent, articulate man with a degree in economics,
social history, and political science, he, less than most,
needed to be told what he should think. Ultimately he
decided in favour of supporting the action of the British
Olympic Association, and he accepted his invitation.

‹ When I decided to go, some people accused me
of being a Communist. Nothing could be further from the
truth. Every athlete has political views, but I do not believe
personal politics should influence one's decision on such a
vital issue. I thought about the matter of Afghanistan at
great length and initially I would say I was sympathetic to
the government line. I believe that you have to support the
elected government, whatever your own political views.
That's democracy. Parliament had voted heavily in favour
of not sending a team, and on other issues I would certainly
argue that we should not go against Parliament. But by
degrees I became disenchanted with the government's
attitude. Without consulting any sports body, such as the
Sports Council, and with no knowledge of, or real interest
in, international sport, the government suddenly sent the
Foreign Secretary to Lausanne to discuss an alternative
Olympics – without any kind of feasibility study. I
considered it was an insult, that with a national budget for
sport of some fifteen million pounds, it was suddenly
possible, at a stroke, to find fifty-five million pounds for an
alternative Olympics in London. I came from a city where
there was not even a single all-weather running track, and I
regarded the government's attitude as totally political
rather than strategic.

I was also anxious that any government, Conservative or
Labour, should not initiate sporting sanctions for some
short-term political pay-off. After that, nothing in sport
would have been sacred, and international sport – the
World Cup in soccer or anything else – would have been
placed in an impossible position. *If* the government
recommended a package which included trade, cultural,

96   RUNNING FREE

and social boycotts as well as sporting ones, I would not
have been happy but I would have supported it. But to
select just two hundred international sportsmen and make
them a persecuted minority was the cheapest form of
political one-upmanship. Nor did you have to be particularly astute politically to realize that America and West
Germany, the two main western countries favouring the
boycott, were involved in elections, and the existing leaders, Carter and Schmidt, were faced by right wing opponents Reagan and Strauss. In both instances the leaders
were probably looking for some political focus, and I
didn't feel we should get caught up in this political stunt.
Of course I had sympathy for Afghanistan's plight, and
with that of Hungary and Czechoslovakia in the past, but I
needed to be sure that any action on my part was going to
make some difference. And I do not think one should
overlook the point made by Enoch Powell: that the government could not compel unless they had the will of the
people, or an act of legislation, and they had neither. The
country was split 70-30 against the boycott.**

━━━━━━━━━━

Seb's early season build-up on the track was quiet and
relatively inconspicuous, a 3,000 metres here, a 1,500
metres there, a 5,000 metres in the Yorkshire Championships at Cudworth in a bitterly cold wind where he ran
outside fourteen minutes. But towards the end of May he
began to sharpen, with a 1:45·4 in the Inter-Counties and,
on 5 June, a 1:44·98 for Loughborough against the AAA,
on cinders. This was followed by a 1:44·7 in the Northern
Counties. All satisfactory, on the face of it, but what the
public did not know was that he was beginning to be
severely troubled by a sore hamstring – the result of something even more critical: sciatic nerve trouble due to frac-
tional displacement of the pelvic girdle over a long period.

━━━━━━━━━━

   **It had been troubling me on and off in the first
few races of the season and on 14 May, following Cud-

worth, I'd had to pull out of a Loughborough match at the
moment I was warming up before the race. It was four
days after this that Steve issued his 'challenge', while he
was running down in Wales, for the meeting at Crystal
Palace on 21 May. The outcome of all that, inevitably,
was that we switched events, he ran the 1,500 metres, I
ran the 800 metres. The injury was beginning to be rather
disturbing, only weeks away from Moscow. I'd originally
had treatment back in 1979, before the records, from
Terry Moule, the osteopath who got Gerry Francis playing
again for Queens Park Rangers, and who sorted out the
back problem of Roger Uttley, the England rugby
forward. Terry believes that in the main all muscle problems have a structural beginning, unless they are sprinters'
pulls or collision injuries. He'd already talked of my
having a tilt of the pelvis. On and off in June, I was also
having treatment from Eddie Franklin, the 'physio' at
Chelsea, who was doing a fine job of keeping the hamstring flexible. I played quite a lot of tennis with Ian Hague
over a couple of months at this time, and had difficulty
stretching for low balls. By the beginning of July it was
beginning to cross my mind that I might not make it to
the Games.

On 27 June, running in the Talbot Games at Crystal
Palace, Ovett took over the 1980 world rankings for 1,500
metres with a time of 3:35·3, the fourth fastest of his
career. He was hard pressed down the finishing straight by
Steve Cram, whose 3:35·6, at nineteen years eight months,
was the world's fastest by a teenager. A few days later the
two great British rivals, Ovett and Coe, set off for Oslo
and the Bislet Games. In what had been a bid for Coe's
1,500 metres record at Crystal Palace, Ovett had been
unsuccessfully paced by Bob Benn and Britain's third
Olympic 800 metres runner, young Dave Warren from
Essex. Before Oslo, Warren had told John Rodda of *The
Guardian* and me that he would not agree to pace Ovett
again in the Bislet Mile, but when we arrived at the

Panorama Hotel it was to discover that pressure had been put on Warren by Andy Norman to make the pace once again.

Coe was going for his fourth world record, the American Wohlhuter's 1,000 metres. I knew of his hamstring problem, which I had not disclosed, and I knew likewise of an exceptional 600 metres in training. For the first time, too, Angela would be there to watch her son in a world record bid. On another glorious Norwegian summer evening both runners delivered the goods. Seb had selected the 1,000 metres to make it a unique four-in-a-row, from 800 metres to the mile, and his first question when I met him at the airport, where I had arrived from a meeting in provincial Norway the previous day, was, 'what's the programme tomorrow?' I was able to tell him that his race was the earlier by an hour, so that even if Ovett was now successful in his bid for the mile, Seb had the chance to be the possessor of all four records for that hour. On the morning of the race we had a stroll around the lake, and Seb explained that his intention was to run the first 800 metres fast and then hang on, rather than save anything for the final 200 metres and finish the race not having expended everything. Wohlhuter's 2:13·9 was considered a 'hard' record; he had passed the 800 metres en route in 1:46·8, and Seb was now aiming for something around 1:46. Although he had eased the problem in his leg for the moment, he was still suffering from the after effects of a heavy cold and throat infection, for which he had been taking antibiotics, and had had to cancel a race in Sweden the previous week.

The start was ridiculously fast: Mike Solomon, Trinidad's Moscow 400 metres representative, went off at such a pace that Bob Casselman, the American hurdler who had been put in by the organizers to take the first leg, could not even get to the front! Solomon went through the 400 metres in 50·1, and Coe in 51, which was pace for an 800 metres record, never mind the 1,000 metres. With a lap to go Coe was out on his own, thirty metres ahead of his old rival Wulbeck, needing a 56 to break the record. He went through the 800 metres in

1:45·2 (the fourth fastest time of the year!) and was now in trouble with his breathing, with Wulbeck gaining ground. Coe gritted his teeth and, looking more strained than in any of his previous three records, held on for his fourth in 2:13·4, with Wulbeck still ten yards down. As he set off on a lap of honour, he shared with Rono a rare distinction of a 'simultaneous' quartet.

———

❝I was pleased, because I wasn't well. In a way it was harder than running a hard 1,500 metres. We only decided finally to go for the record once we knew that Maina wasn't in the field, and we decided to make it fast for the first two laps because physiological information we had about Wulbeck, from tests in Germany, suggested he would find it hardest that way. I didn't hear the 800 metres time, but I knew from the pace Solomon had set that it must be quick, and that I would really have to start working over the last 200 metres. I tied up badly between 130 and 80 metres out, and then I managed to get fluid again. But for the cold I think I could have run 2:12, but at least I'd done it with my mother watching. I'd given her a little something back for all those months and years of patience and attention she had given me. As I ran the lap of honour, I could see her up in the stand sitting next to John Walker's wife. For a few hours afterwards my system was really turned upside down, I was very sick. Whatever doctors say, antibiotics affect your system physically. But however grotty I was feeling temporarily, it was a good finish to my Olympic preparation.❞

———

It was with rare expectation that the Bislet crowd awaited Ovett's appearance. They were not disappointed. Warren took the field through the first quarter in 55·5, with Ovett slotted in behind. In fourth and fifth position Steve Cram and Graham Williamson were locked in a duel to decide which of them would be Britain's third runner in the Moscow 1,500 metres, one of the last vacancies in the track

and field team. Warren led Ovett through the half-way
mark in 1:53·5, and Williamson, who throughout the season was beset by one misfortune after another, had
already fallen away. Ovett's two-lap time of 1:53·8 put
him one and a half seconds ahead of Coe's pace in the
record run the previous year; and a 57 third lap left him
no less than 2·4 seconds in front of Coe's time at the same
stage. Warren had dropped out with 600 metres to go,
obliging Ovett to go to the front. Looking in superb shape
all the way to the tape, Ovett was home in what seemed
to be a new record. But was it?

Unaccountably, for the only time in more than twenty
races in the meeting, the electronic timing apparatus had
stalled. It was said later that the starter's gun had failed to
activate the clock, so the judges were dependent on the
back-up timing of hand-held watches. After a long delay
the time was announced as 3:48·8, a fifth of a second
inside Coe's record. But would electronic timing, always
considered to be fractionally faster in activation and therefore producing a slower time, still have given him the
record? The many international journalists present
debated the matter into the early hours of the morning.
What was certain was that, under IAAF regulations then
in force, Ovett's time would be recognized – and that he
and Coe were heading for one hell of a confrontation in
Moscow.

———

‘Of course I was disappointed, but I wasn't shat-
tered; I didn't feel I'd lost a part of me, and it wasn't quite
the blow I'd felt it had been to John Walker the previous
year. I watched with Peter, and when 2:51 came up for
the three-quarter-mile, he thought Steve would really rup-
ture the record by a couple of seconds. Steve and I had a
brief talk afterwards, I told him I'd enjoyed his race and
he thanked me but said he hadn't seen mine because
he was warming up. As far as I was concerned, it was
irrelevant who held the record when it came to the
Olympic 1,500 metres. The record was only borrowed for

Steve, the same as it was for me. People questioned me indirectly after Steve's record in the following days, as much as to say, 'what are you going to do about that?' But I never doubted that he was capable of it, I was sure he had been for some time. What mattered to me, at that stage in Oslo, was my own confidence in winning in Moscow, whether the 1,500 metres was run at 3:37 pace or 3:28. I was encouraged by the fact that both Walker and his coach Arch Jelley told me they felt I would win. 9

═════════

Adrian Metcalfe was less certain. His closing message to ITV viewers back home in Britain was, 'well, I leave you with a comparison of the last 200 metres of the two races, and ask yourself who is looking the easier . . .'. Two weeks later Ovett returned to Bislet for yet another record attempt, this time on Seb's 1,500 metres mark, with the Olympics less than a week away. He now stoked the flames even higher for the meetings in Moscow by equalling Coe's record. This time the electronic clock was working, and Ovett crossed the line at the end of a fierce race with Wessinghage, Walker, and Lacey, in 3:32·09. That was six hundredths of a second slower than Seb's Zürich record, but both rounded up to the same 3:32·1. If neither improved on their times before the IAAF introduced records measured to a hundredth in January 1981, Seb's would stand as the faster. The two remarkable Britons entered the Games with two records each and one shared: Seb the 800 metres and 1,000 metres, Steve the mile and two miles, the 1,500 metres held jointly; the prelude to a riveting showdown.

═════════

6 I wouldn't have wanted a race so close to the Games, it was a break from training routine for Steve at a time when training was in my opinion more important. He claimed he wanted the psychological advantage of it. Things were brewing up for a good series of races in Moscow. 9

6: A Race without History

A rainbow of flags, like balloons at a children's party, fluttered from every lamp post, beckoning us to suspend all thought of reality. Once we had run the gauntlet of unsmiling immigration inspection, we were expected to be seduced by Moscow's lavish party, so much of it as artificial as the cardboard wedding cake in the baker's window. The 1980 Olympics, once they began, were, as always, made by the athletes, not by the city in which they happened to be. As one walked through the Village gates once more, Baron de Coubertin's now almost extinct ideology of *taking part* was still there in the air, a concept which, however much it may have been eroded by politics, professionalism, and the use of drugs, still carries faintly the old alchemy of a common pursuit of excellence. Of course, in one sense, the whole thing was a stupendous absurdity, a giant stewpot of vested interests in which the Killanin-led administration was dwarfed and overrun by its own vehicle. Yet, although the 1979 Soviet Government official handbook for Party Activists might claim, 'to decide to hold the Games in Moscow is convincing proof of the recognition of the correctness of our country's foreign policy', there would be few competitors who would believe this preposterous claim for a moment.

There were many visitors to the Games, including competitors, who came and went without ever sensing or seeing the dark side of Soviet life. The city had been laundered for the occasion. Dissidents, drunks, most cars, and children under sixteen had been evacuated, their places taken by the thousands of extra police who hovered every five yards on every street, even hiding in the bushes, ensuring that there was the minimum contact between the ordinary Russian and any visitor from the West. The hundreds of officials required to administer the Games, from stadium stewards to waitresses, would not fraternize one jot beyond the formal necessities of doing their job – which is not to say that in most instances the job was not done exceptionally well. That is why some unquestioning visitors left with the impression that the Russians have the sun shining out of their hearts. Sadly, that is precisely the point. Many of them do, but they are bound, in every action they take, by the most comprehensive totalitarian régime ever known to man. By the time the three weeks were drawing to a close, some of the formality had melted. Off duty, unobserved in the back of a bus with his beret off, the Russian 'squaddie' was no different from one anywhere else in the world: interested in a chat, a beer, a laugh, a fag, and a pretty girl. I know because I met them. It was the same with the translators in the hotels and press centres, with the concierges who monitor every floor of every hotel, enthroned like plebeian Queen Victorias behind their desks, dispensing room keys and tea at any hour of the day or night and, in consequence, all-seeing. But beneath an adopted severity many of them were as gentle as any granny. It is the system, not the human beings who comprise it, which is depressing – show your identification to pass through every door, to mount every bus; if you go out of the hotel front door to speak to a colleague standing on the pavement, return by *another* door through electronic scrutiny back into a hotel where there is nobody but journalists anyway! 'Marry me' said a hostess in the Lenin Stadium press centre with a sardonic laugh, as she chastely handed me the latest information sheet from the computer, 'and I promise to

leave you the moment I step foot in London!' She, and a
million others.

═══════════

6 As we came in to land, the British Airways pilot
said over the intercom: 'Ladies and gentlemen, we are
about to arrive in Moscow. Enjoy yourselves!' There was
a wave of laughter. As we taxied in, you could see line
upon line of civil aircraft, as if the Russians were anxious
to show us their new prosperity. We came into the vast,
empty arrival hall, like some huge cardboard cut-out, soul-
less in its emptiness. There was all hell let loose the other
side of customs. As we boarded a bus, Alan Pascoe put an
arm round me and said, 'well, I hope you can get some
peace and quiet now you're here'. I don't think he realized the irony of that. Daley was lapping it all up as usual,
adoring the attention. As we left the plane, a stewardess
had given me a couple of plastic bags of mini tins of
orange juice. Daley had grabbed them, saying he needed
them for his ten events, Brendan joked that he could get
a house for them in Moscow. We were the usual happy,
laughing bunch of sportsmen arriving before a big event.
Brendan was a bit smug that he was no longer the centre
of attention, that he wasn't obliged to perform for the
cameras.

I had set off prepared for the same as in Prague: to
queue in Moscow, to have to wait for food, and not to be
all that happy. But once I arrived in the Village I was very
impressed with the rooms, and the space, though there
was more room in the Village, in terms of the accommo-
dation, because of the boycott, of course. The security was
oppressive, but you just had to bear with it; and they'd
painstakingly searched all my books at the airport. The
food turned out to be superb, huge amounts of everything
you could want: steaks, fish, fruit, cereals – most of it
imported, of course – and one heard that the Russians had
gone without many things in the preceding months so as
to provide for the Games. The East Europeans had clearly
seen nothing like it for ages, you'd see Bulgarian weight-

lifters leaving the self-service counter with whole trays of oranges and bananas. It was a pleasant surprise to find that the living conditions were not going to be a hassle.

My preparation had gone as well as I could have hoped; apart from the hamstring I was as fit as I'd ever been. It was Sunday, I wasn't racing till Thursday, and I could relax a bit. Yet there was also a strange, almost hollow feeling, knowing that for the duration of the Games, for the next two weeks, this was your world, you wouldn't be going anywhere else other than to the Stadium, and that at the end of the two weeks all the speculation and questions would be answered. I found myself looking at people and wondering how they would react, what they would be saying to each other if I came away with nothing. In the artificial surroundings of a Village, you cannot be yourself, on your own: whether you like it or not you are thrust upon other people to an extent, and they on you, and you start getting caught up in their feelings, the way I suppose it must be among the crew of a submarine. **9**

The only practical irritation on arrival had been that British Airways had given substance to the apocryphal slogan 'Breakfast in London, Lunch in Moscow, Luggage in Tokyo' by losing a grip containing all Seb's training gear. Luckily his running spikes had been in a small bag which he never allows out of his sight. While BA went hunting – 'Hello, is that Siberian lost property?' – Seb hurried off to the most heavily attended press conference in the history of the Olympics. It was the intention of David Shaw that such a conference would give the world's press the opportunity to question the triple world record holder at the first available moment, and thereafter allow him some peace. Interest in the Rossiya Hotel – a self-contained block the size of Green Park, with 6,000 beds, where the entire written press was housed in 'quarantine' away from the locals – had been fuelled by Ovett's interview two days previously, in which he had stated that he had a fifty per cent chance in the 800 metres and a ninety per cent chance in the 1,500 metres. But the gathering of 400 or more press and TV men was kept waiting in the main press centre lecture room in central Moscow for over forty-five minutes.

The cause of this delay was symptomatic of the red tape which was to drive some of us almost to resignation in the coming weeks. Because neither Seb nor Peter were accredited journalists, they required, believe it or not, elaborate separate accreditation to enter the press centre! And the authorities had got themselves in a twist over Peter and Percy. Peter's real name is in fact Percy, duly entered in his passport, but some sharp-nosed bureaucrat had spotted that his Olympic accreditation was in the name of Peter. Ah, zo, a plot! It took almost an hour for the error to be acknowledged as such, corrected, and approved, after which the world's foremost athlete and his coach were at liberty to meet the press. Seb, reasonably relaxed, tactfully deflected barbed questions. No, he wasn't under instructions not to answer political questions, his views were already well known and he was now here exclusively to run. Yes, he was pleasantly surprised with the Village and the excellence of the food. Yes, he would definitely run both the 800 metres and 1,500 metres, contrary to rumours going round the press hotel. No, in answer to an East German, he did not think he and Ovett would be running as a team! No, in answer to Ovett's allegation that he was a 'programmed' athlete, his training was not that hard and was less than that of some others. Yes, he hoped Bayi would be in good shape for the 1,500 metres, 'because we want it to be a fast race of which we can all be proud'. Did Ovett really think he had a ninety per cent chance in the 1,500 metres; if he did he must have a crystal ball. No, in answer to a Finn, he had no detailed knowledge of the East German or Soviet runners, but he didn't prepare for races with individuals in mind. No, he wasn't worried by Ovett's recent records, he had always believed Ovett had the ability. Tass, the Soviet news agency, asked enigmatically what his feelings were as a human being, now he was in Moscow. Seb, equally enigmatically, said he felt 'an element of excitement'. Didn't we all!

‛I was a little bit worried that I would give the impression that I was holding court, doing an Ali, which was exactly what a German asked: 'Why are you here?' But, looking back, the press conference was a good thing and when I went to the training track that afternoon I was able to say to journalists who wanted to interrupt that I had already answered all the questions I was able to The British team officials, Nick Whitehead and Lynn Davies, kept off the photographers.

I hadn't heard about Steve's prediction till I arrived at the press conference. We travelled on the Sunday and I missed the papers. My first thought was, is he confident or insecure? What *are* the implications when you suddenly open up to a newspaper after systematically refusing to talk to the press for several years? He could have said what he said to any of the regular athletics writers, and he would have received good coverage, so when he suddenly talked to a paper which does not regularly give much attention to athletics, you have to wonder why. Apart from any other consideration, his exclusive interviews with a Sunday paper and with ITV were contraventions of the Olympic charter, which states that while a competitor is not obliged to give interviews, if he does he should be available to all sources. I was left with the feeling that he had probably been used, that his feelings had been over-stated for the benefit of the paper's 'exclusive'. In fact, Steve and I were on very good terms in Moscow. We had sympathy for each other, knowing that the eyes of the world were on us, that it was some kind of Judgement Day, that whether or not we both won gold medals people would make distinctions and overload them upon us. I have a tremendous respect for his athletic ability, he is one of the most talented runners there's ever been, and his range, from 400 metres to a half-marathon, is unsurpassed.

The days leading up to the heats of the 800 metres were uneventful, I was relaxed, sleeping soundly, moving well on the track, and the hamstring was easing. I felt my condition was improving with every day I was there, my heavy cold from Oslo had cleared, and the sun was doing me a power of good – I was delighted when it really became scorchingly hot the day before the 800 metres heats. I was conscious of pressure, but at this stage it was an abstract thing. I'd felt it most, in a strange way, when I went down with Peter to inspect the track; standing there in the empty Lenin Stadium, where the action would all happen for the first time I suddenly began to grasp the enormity of the occasion. Yet I liked the track, it was not too hard, the curves were good, the whole place had a mood of drama even when empty. All in all, I felt confident that I could cope with whatever was thrown at me in the next few days. Speed hurts, sustained speed kills, on the track; and from my experience of the world records at 800 metres and 1,000 metres, I felt that I could, if necessary, sustain something faster than anyone else.'

By the time the six 800 metres heats were completed, the thought crossed my mind that the East Germans were in a possible position to run a team race in the final. Andreas Busse, Olaf Beyer (the Prague champion), and Detlef Wagenknecht (referred to among the British as Wagon Wheels for simplification) were all tall and powerful, and it was certainly on the cards that they could make a team decision as to who had the strongest individual chance, and then get the other two to gang up on the British, tactically. Busse, second to Seb in the rankings prior to the Games, looked particularly impressive, as did Nikki Kirov, the powerful little Russian in a blood red vest. Ovett began the saga with an untroubled 1:49·39 in the opening heat, then came Wagenknecht and Kirov with a joint 1:47·5, followed by Busse with 1:47·34. Seb, coasting wide in fourth place at the bell – 'like running in a greenhouse', as Mike McLeod, Britain's 10,000 metres runner, said – had an easy 1:48·43, marginally faster than Beyer in Heat Five, with Dave Warren comfortably home in the sixth and slowest heat. With the first three from each heat and the six fastest among the losers qualifying for the three semi-finals, it had been simple enough for the fast men. The semis would be tougher, with only the first two and the two fastest losers reaching the final. The draw put Seb in the third semi, with only 'Wagon Wheels' likely to offer any challenge to him at that stage.

━━━━━━━

‘There was no problem: I was relaxed, ran wide down the first back straight to keep out of trouble, was nicely placed in third position at the bell, and pulled ahead of Wagenknecht in the last 70 metres, after holding onto his surge round the final bend. We were given the same time, and I now felt that he was the main threat amongst the East Germans. Beyer had unexpectedly gone out in the second semi, fourth behind Kirov, Dave Warren, and Marajo of France. My time, and Kirov's and Steve's in the first semi, were almost identical, and my feeling about the final was no different from before the Games started. I considered I was sufficiently improved to cope with whatever cropped up, leaving aside the fact of my record being a second faster than anyone else had ever run. We'd discussed the possibility of running from the front, but considered that there was a far greater chance in an Olympic final, where anyone can be inspired on the day to do something far beyond their previous form, to do all the work for just such a runner and then get stuffed on the run-in. Not that we considered it *would* happen, and certainly the temptation was there. I could probably have got away with it, keeping clear of the bargeing and spiking, avoiding being boxed or forced to run wide. But ultimately we decided, on the assumption of my having the fastest basic speed, that the safest race was still to hold back, sit in on the pace of the leaders, cover anything that happened up front, and kick somewhere round the last bend. We knew I had the speed over 150 metres for it not to be a risk, and the faster the early race, the more I should have in hand, relative to the others, in the final stages.’

The semi-final times had been nothing special, and Seb would start the final even more a favourite than Juantorena in Montreal. The draw the night before had placed him in the outside lane of the eight runners, giving him all the options, and none of the dangers of having opponents cut across him in the sprint for the second bend after the lane-break following the first bend. I still believed he should run from the front, but it was none of my business, and I respected his and Peter's judgement enough to prevent me throwing in gratuitous doubts from my position of a privileged bystander. The draw for the final, with qualifying times and personal bests prior to the Games, was:

	Qualifying time	Personal best
Nikolai Kirov (USSR)	1:46·6	1:45·6
Steve Ovett (GB)	1:46·6	1:44·1
Alberto Guimaraes (Brazil)	1:46·9	1:46·0
Detlef Wagenknecht (GDR)	1:46·7	1:45·9
Dave Warren (GB)	1:47·2	1:46·2
Jose Marajo (France)	1:47·3	1:43·9
Andreas Busse (GDR)	1:46·9	1:44·8
Sebastian Coe (GB)	1:46·7	1:42·4

Peter, without actually being worried, considered that the main threat – Ovett apart – would come from Wagenknecht, and he felt that Marajo, qualifying as a fastest loser, had not shown the sort of form to approach his personal best of 1:43·9. In his heart he knew, and Seb knew, that providing he gave himself the chance, by positioning himself in the right place at the right time, short of injury there could only be one winner. But what was to be the worst day of Seb's young life began badly.

‘I've never known pressure like it. I thought people had exaggerated, but they hadn't. There was no comparison. I'd felt pressure going into the Europa Cup final

the year before, but it just wasn't the same thing. It began
after the semi-final. I can remember looking down into my
food at dinner amid the hubbub of the huge crowded
restaurant, and glancing up and catching Peter's eye. He
must have sensed I was uneasy because he smiled and
said, 'don't start *now*'. It was unusual for me, I'd never
been like that so long before a race. I had the worst
night's sleep I've ever had, just lying there listening to my
own heartbeat, thinking to myself, you've coped with the
pressure all year, for heaven's sake take a grip! But it was
the same next day. At lunch I knocked over my orange
juice, and then dropped the cream carton into my cup of
coffee. I suddenly felt ungainly, conscious of my own
awkwardness. That morning I'd seen Kenny Mays of the
Daily Telegraph, and he'd said with that friendly leer of
his, 'well, 7.30 tonight, the moment I've been waiting for'.
The moment *he* had been waiting for! It was just the kind
of well-meant comment that tightens your nerves another
turn. In the afternoon I couldn't sleep again, which is rare
for me. Peter was up in the room, and he knew what was
going on, but he knew that saying anything wouldn't help.

I can remember the relief of getting on the move at last,
going down to the stadium. But leaving the Village my
attitude was all wrong. I wanted to hurry into the warm
up, I didn't want to be alone. I'd already gone through the
nervous bit, and now I was detached, disconnected. Mentally, I was an hour ahead of schedule. Normally, the
detached phase happens in the few minutes before the
race, when you've done the physical and mental wind-up
and you're ready to cut out everything: voices, faces,
sounds. But I was like this with forty-five minutes still to
go. The race had that written all over it, it was a disinterested race, someone going through the motions. After
the warm up there was the long walk over the bridge to
the main stadium. Steve had looked tense. He and Harry
were together ahead of Peter and me, with the British
team managers at the back. They wished us good luck,
and we went down into the little preparation room where
we got our lane numbers for our shorts, and they checked
the number and length of our spikes.❜

As Peter watched Seb disappear into the bowels of the
stadium he was aware that all was not well with his athlete, as he had been for some time. His problem was that
he was not really sure *what* was wrong, nor how best to
correct it. Many weeks later, turning the race over in his
mind for the hundredth time, he would admit to me:

'I have to ask myself why, of all times, did I not prepare
him properly – *if* I didn't? I had always said that if he
lost it would be my fault. That's why, afterwards, I was
ashamed. For myself. I had sensed for a while before
the final that he was detached, almost inert, but I was
alert to the danger of putting *more* pressure on him. He
doesn't like me to bother him in the hour before a big
race. Our work together has by then been done, and
he's locked into himself in mental preparation. In that
last hour I'm just a valet. My suggesting he might be
about to lose was the last thing he needed. I couldn't
think what I should do, but getting it wrong could have
been even worse than doing nothing. My fear was to
undermine him, even knowing he was not properly
switched on. The point was that at 800 metres he had to
be *so* bad to lose, I couldn't conceive that, even though
he was a shade sluggish, he would blow it. I must have
supposed subconsciously that he would still be OK. I
knew he was, at his best, immeasurably better than anyone else in the race. It was nonsense to suggest, as
David Coleman did in the Sportsview Personality of the
Year programme, that Seb was tactically naïve. He had
proved himself in some hard races, without me. What I
didn't know at that moment before the 800 metres was
how to say something to sharpen him without creating
doubt. I could imagine him looking at me and saying,
"Christ, what a thing to say to me at this moment!" So
I said nothing.'

The relationship between a great athlete and his coach,
however stable in times of calm, can be as volatile as a
love affair when under pressure.

‘ I'd changed my official-issue vest because the seams had been chafing, and had had my race number, 254 – the same throughout the Games – restitched onto the old GB shirt in which I had broken the world records. Over at the warm up track the two East Germans had been striding together, so had Steve and Dave, and it vaguely crossed my mind that they might have planned something together. But then I realized that on balance this was silly; I couldn't believe that anyone would go into an Olympic final and sacrifice his own chance for someone else. Besides, I consoled myself, it was not now in Steve's interest to have a fast early pace. I was beginning to be a little more keyed up, but I still wasn't mentally right. The wretched business of being made to walk everywhere in single file in lane order irked me, and I took a delight now, and again in the 1,500 metres final, in breaking rank. We filed out past the window of the kitchens under the stadium, and I was acutely aware of the rancid, sickly smell. We put our gear in the plastic baskets; I could hear the names being called out over the loud-speakers. We were allowed a brief warm up on the track, had to go back into the tunnel afterwards, then out again once more in lane order to the start. Going to the line I can only remember feeling utterly empty. For me the race would be memorable only for the little I could remember about it afterwards. As we waited in the tunnel, Steve had said to me: 'It's stupid to think we're doing this here for nothing, when we could turn professional and fill a stadium on our own.' ’

It was cooler than it had been in the past few days, and the flags around the rim of the stadium were stiffening in a strong wind which did not penetrate down as far as the runners. Already the floodlights were on in the half light of the evening. As the runners went to the line Sara Simeone, who had obliged Seb to dodge round her during the warm up, dislodged the bar in the women's high jump. The moment the gun went Seb moved off as if it was the start of a 10,000 metres race. I couldn't believe it. He looked as if he was running in soft sand. At the lane break, it was Guimaraes of Brazil leading from Kirov, and as they approached the second bend Ovett was badly boxed as the runners converged in front of him, coming across from the outside, while he attempted to hold his ground in the second lane where he had begun. Coming off the first bend, Seb had made no attempt to accelerate and close on the leaders; in the next few seconds that seemed no bad thing.

❲I remember the gun going and feeling sluggish, running without conviction. There was so much that was adrift. I came off the lane break after 130 metres with no awareness of anyone's positions. I was thinking of *nothing*! Going into the second bend I was probably in my best position in the race, fifth or sixth, with Ovett just in front of me.❳

It was now that Ovett vigorously handed off Wagenknecht. The 6 foot 4 inch East German lost his balance and, in attempting to stay on his feet, veered outwards and, in turn, impeded Marajo, who almost went down. A few strides further on, Ovett swerved to the right, and again Marajo was impeded. Coming into the home straight for the first time, Guimaraes was still in the lead but with the entire field still bunched together within three strides, Seb loping along on the outside at the back, with Ovett caught with a wall of runners in front of him. Approaching the bell, Ovett tried to force his way between Wagenknecht and Kirov – and failed. As Guimaraes went through the half way in 54·5, Ovett was sixth, and Seb last.

‘Running wide off the second bend, and wide down the straight, I was conscious of being last at the bell but I still had a total lack of urgency, perhaps because the field was so bunched. What I had no awareness of was how hopelessly compromised Steve was at that stage. When I saw the video I realized it was one of the several opportunities I had to make a decisive move. Instead, I continued to run wide round the third bend.’

Here Warren made a burst to the front past the Brazilian; Kirov following, with Ovett accelerating out of the bend to keep in touch. Still Seb failed to react. Going into the final bend Kirov went past Warren and, with 200 metres to go, led Ovett by a couple of strides, with Guimaraes and Wagenknecht another two strides down on Ovett, and Coe, Busse, and Marajo together another three metres down.

‘Down the back straight I still felt, erroneously, that I was OK; I was aware that Kirov had surged, but until we turned into the bend I wasn't aware how much, because of the runners in between. Into the final bend I still hadn't been buried, but I hung back as Busse and Marajo went by.’

It was allowing himself to be boxed at this moment which finally cost Seb the race. By the time he changed gear and moved outside the others, he was some twelve to thirteen metres, or about six strides, adrift of the leader. Coming off the final bend Ovett made his move and overtook Kirov. Way back, Seb was at last responding. Knowing in my heart it was a vain hope even for Seb, I turned to Ian

Wooldridge of the *Daily Mail*, high up in the press box, and said, 'here he comes!' Seb ripped past Busse and Marajo, then the fading Wagenknecht and Guimaraes. With forty metres to go he was third and still gaining on Kirov and Ovett. With twenty metres to go he passed Kirov, but now his astonishing sprint was spent and in the last few strides he could close no further on Ovett. By a substantial three metres the gold medal was Ovett's in 1:45·4.

＝＝＝＝＝＝

‘When Steve made his move off the final bend he was about five strides up, and by the time I reacted to get clear of Busse and Marajo, Steve must have been eight strides up. That's fifteen metres. Entering the final straight, I knew that I'd probably blown it, that it was going to mean a fantastic effort to pull back. Suddenly I was going past people. One went, and I was fifth; two more, and I was third and overhauling Kirov. I wondered if I was even going to get a medal. I didn't know how well I'd run the last 150 metres until I came into the press conference half an hour later and you, David, said, 'like a train', and I thought 'Oh God!'. I'd grown accustomed to taking liberties in one or two races in the last year, to running wide from the back, and now, in the most devastating way, I'd discovered you can't do that in an Olympic final. I wasted so much nervous energy before the race, I'd never been as nervous before, yet look at the chances the race still gave me! Going into the final bend I thought I was in contention, then suddenly realized it was a hell of a gap and that I was going to have to run myself out even to get a medal.

With thirty metres to go I knew I was not going to win. At the finish I just went off the track and the extraordinary thing was that my first reaction was a huge feeling of relief rather than disappointment. That it was *over*. I went into the doping test room still uninterested. Sara Simeone was there, crying, having just won her gold. I was reacting in the same way as people often do after a car accident,

wanting only to get away from the scene. Steve was cough-
ing and looked fatigued. I was in and out of the dope
test in minutes . . . and I'd lost. It told me just how much
I'd failed to use my strength on the track.

As we came out for the medal ceremony it was at last
beginning to sink in, the size of the disaster. There was
the incessant clicking of cameras: will you and Steve shake
hands, will you shake your fist over his head, will
you . . . will you . . . . Up on the rostrum I *did* shake
Steve's hand. Clive James in *The Observer* wrote that I
looked as if I'd just been handed a turd, which was a bit
harsh; I don't think I was discourteous to Steve. I was just
blank, I didn't hear the Olympic hymn as the Olympic flags
were raised, or notice the re-run of the finish on the giant
electronic screen. At the time, and since the Games, a
few people have said that I looked grim and seemed less
than generous in defeat. But it had nothing to do with losing to Steve, I was just totally disconnected, I knew I had
run appallingly in what was supposed to be *my* event, and
the numbness would have been the same whoever had
won. That rostrum was no place to be smiling after tossing
the race away.

Back in the tunnel I was sitting in a chair with my head
in my hands. Mike Murphy of BBC TV came up to me in
a friendly way, and with that aggressive forefinger push of
his glasses on the bridge of his nose, said, 'get your f_____
head up, Coe'. He meant well, knowing I had to pull
myself together for the 1,500 metres. But both the press
and TV had wanted me to win because of Steve's refusal
to co-operate with them, they wanted it as much for themselves as for me, I suspected. If I'd lost to Walker or Bayi
or Scott, the media wouldn't have put the same pressure
on me as they did now. It was an added burden I didn't
need. 〉

═══════════

Up in the press and commentary boxes, many were waiting for a protest by either the East Germans or the
French. Whether or not it might have been upheld, it

never came. Twice, at 200 metres and again at 450
metres, Ovett had, in the words of Cliff Temple in *The Sunday Times*, 'almost literally fought his way out of trouble'.
Chris Brasher said in *The Observer*, 'it was perilously close
to the rules', while the authoritative *Athletics Weekly*'s
Mel Watman claimed: 'Ovett ran so physical a race that
he can consider himself lucky not to have been disqualified.' Ovett himself would admit in an interview for ITV
with Metcalfe: 'If anyone was guilty of doing more than
their fair share of pushing, it was probably me. I can be
called the worst of the bunch, but I honestly believe that
everyone ran a fair race. People were wearing half-inch
spikes, and if anyone gets close to you, you fend them off
because they are dangerous. It looks as if you're pushing,
but it's safety precautions.' Henry Cooper, giving his considered view on television, said in his inimitable cockney
vernacular: 'The difference was between one geeser 'oo
knew 'ow to use 'is elbows, and one 'oo didn't. Blimey, I
thought athletics was a gen'lman's sport!' Neil Amdur, a
droll New Yorker who knows the athletics scene inti-
mately, said as we filed down to the interview room in
Moscow: 'It was a race without history.'

    ❛Only after I'd seen the video did I realize how
physical Steve had been. I felt it had contributed to the
tattiness of the race. It lowered the standing of athletics. I
was very surprised the East Germans and French didn't
make more of it. I would hate to think that as a result of
that final we might breed a race of middle-distance runners who breast-stroke their way out of a scrum. The 800
metres is unique, because nowadays it is almost a sprint
the whole way, just not in lanes for the last 670 metres.
It's eight guys fighting for position in a sprint spread over
two-and-a-half lanes. Of course you have to react tactically, and I didn't. But if you accept the development of
physical contact, then tactics mean nothing, and the
roughest man is going to win. You cannot equate racing
ability with handing people off, as some of the press did.

It is tactically allowable to protect the space you have earned by your pace or your positioning, but *not* to gain space that is occupied by somebody else which you would prefer. That is not tactical intelligence, it's the negation of it. **)**

———

Ovett, as in Prague, declined to attend the official press conference. When Seb arrived, more with the air of an eight-year-old who has just been pulled out of the canal than an Olympic silver medalist, Peter was already sitting there at the table alongside the Master of Ceremonies. By facing up to the world's press after such a personal howler, Seb was showing considerably more nerve than he had in the race. As he took his seat Peter, who had not yet spoken to him, whispered in his ear, 'you ran like an idiot', though his face contained not a trace of criticism. Still in a daze, Seb answered the battery of questions: yes, I made tactical errors; no, I didn't respond at the right moments; my intention was to do nothing more than anyone else did at the front and to cover the breaks, but I didn't; obviously there was a lot of pressure but at this level you have to expect it . . . .

———

(It was like an autopsy in there. Malcolm Brammer from Sheffield was in tears, Neil Allen looked awful. Colin Hart's (athletics correspondent of *The Sun*) face suggested he'd lost a pile. Peter was very good, he didn't need to tell me how badly I'd run. I knew all too well, and I knew how hard I'd hit him. **)**

———

Father and son battled their way through the crush of reporters and down the steps of the stadium to look for their official car back to the Village. Outside it was dark. Peter put his arm round Seb, Malcolm was on the other side of him. I muttered to Peter, 'quickly, there's a camera

unit after him', as a hand-held camera and sound man
tried to get round in front of them. Seb was shaking, close
to tears: they were tears of anger more than disappointment. Behind us, looming out of the darkness, padded Jim
Lawton, a former *Express* colleague now working in Van-
couver. Jim, always a sensitive writer, had seen all he
needed to know from some yards off, and discreetly
turned back towards the press room.

We found the car, after first going to the wrong warm-
up track. As we crossed the bridge for the second time,
Seb asked bitterly, 'how much did I make up?' I said ten
metres. 'Oh, Christ', he said again as the magnitude of his
error sank deeper into his at last conscious brain. We
bundled into the car and the impassive Russian chauffeur
moved off. In his mis-adjusted driving mirror I could see
Peter in the back seat with his arm round Seb, the way
you comfort your infant child when it comes to your bed
in the middle of the night troubled by a nightmare. There
was no recrimination there, only mutual love and shared
grief. It was not a time for talk, and I stared ahead
through the windscreen at the wide, now almost deserted
road back to the Village. On arrival I had to enter by a
different gate. In case I failed to gain admission to join
them for dinner, Seb said, 'thanks for caring', and I said,
'it's disproved nothing, winning the 1,500 metres can now
only be even sweeter'.

⸻

❝I was grateful for the darkness. I kept thinking
why now, why the Olympics, why not Cudworth, or Hull?
I just hadn't believed it could happen to me, and now
suddenly there was this nagging fear: is this, like Prague,
going to be the story of my career, missing out when it
really matters? Back in our block, Mary Peters threw her
arms round me in tears. I had a shower and went to bed.
A few came to the room, Brendan was the first. 'You just
didn't race, did you, you froze.' I felt so stupid, that others
could remember so much about the race and I could
remember almost nothing.❞

I had caught the last bus from the Village back to the centre of Moscow shortly before midnight. I knew that the loneliest woman in Britain at this moment was probably Angela. I took a cab from the press centre back to the Rossiya, and called her on the direct dial telephone from my room, which occasionally worked first time, or could take up to thirty attempts to get through to London depending, I suppose, on what sort of mood eavesdropping Boris was in. Tonight I was lucky. Angela answered: surprised, alarmed. In the past, she had told me previously, she had been dismayed at the apparent ruthlessness of the schedules which her husband had set her son, thinking 'it shouldn't happen to a dog'. She herself came from the sort of background in which you apologized for winning at tennis, but slowly she had become accustomed to the evident streak of aggression in her otherwise shy son. Her first worry now was not that he had lost, but what effect defeat might have had upon him. She longed to be near him, to tell him it was only a *race*. To me she said anxiously: 'How is he, how has he taken it, do you think he'll retire if he doesn't win the 1,500 metres?' 'No,' I said, 'I don't think he'll retire, he's angry as much as disappointed. Give him a day or two and he'll have recovered. I'm doubling all my bets on the 1,500 metres.'

On the sixth floor of the British quarters, son and father hardly slept, talking the night away in a subdued, at times agonized, at times rational, post-mortem. People are apt to say, glibly, that they would give their right arm for something, but when the father now said he would give his for his son's success in the 1,500 metres, I would accept that he truly meant it.

7: Dark Days

‘The next morning when I got up, Daley came bouncing in, full of life as ever. 'What's the weather like?' he asked. 'Looks a bit silver to me', I said. 'I've been thinking,' Daley mused, at his most mischievous, 'after you've won the 1,500 metres, why don't we get a picture of Mrs Ovett with his medal, your Dad with yours, and my Auntie Doreen with mine. The press would just love that!' I laughed, but I didn't feel like laughing. The worst hangover imaginable could not compare with what I felt when I woke up. To rub it in, the celebrations for Allan Wells' gold in the 100 metres had still been going on in the room next door – telegrams arriving, a continuous noise, just as it should have been, but it made it twice as bad for me.

Had winning bred complacency in me? I had possibly felt deep down that the 800 metres would come *to* me, I probably didn't give it enough thought. What I needed now was a good long run to clear my mind and my body, so I left the Village to do ten or eleven miles on the road in under the hour. I was tracked the *whole* way by a carload of British photographers. I know that up to a point it's their job, but I felt they were like vultures. That's irrational, because you like the attention when you've won, when they capture a happy face or a good run. But that morning I felt it was an intrusion. I found out later

DARK DAYS123

that one of the tabloid papers had carried a picture the next morning under the headline 'Trail of Shame'. Fortunately I didn't know about it at the time. I just felt better for the run, resolutely ignoring the unwelcome dawn patrol. '

———————————

The papers back home were fierce in their dismissal of Seb as just one more in the long line of record-breakers who allegedly did not possess the innate racing brain when it came to a major championship final. Peter Hildreth in the *Sunday Telegraph* went even farther, and suggested that Seb had an inherent lack of physical strength for the occasion, saying:

> 'No power on earth can now prevent Ovett from winning the 1,500 metres on Friday. That is, after all, his priority and Coe's weaker distance. Any chance of Coe beating Ovett in the 1,500 metres would have had to follow his establishing a moral ascendancy in the 800 metres which he singularly failed to do. As the pair have not met since two years ago, when Ovett beat Coe for the silver medal in the European Championship, there has been little chance to make a direct comparison. While I do not suggest that either of these outstanding runners takes anabolic steroids or any other drugs, the palpable contrast between them in general physical profile and musculature is an object lesson.'

John Rodda of *The Guardian*, who has seen more athletics than most and, in collaboration with Lord Killanin, was the author of a history of the Olympics, was dismissive of both Seb and the race itself:

> 'The first instalment of the Coe v Ovett saga was a bad ticket-seller for the next. . . . Ovett won and why he did not wave an arm down the finishing straight I do not know, unless it is that he has some respect for the dignity of even these Olympic Games. In the event he won

the race as though he were on the athletic circus somewhere, turning out a performance against a gathering of
well-meaning locals. It was a flat, anti-climactic affair
that was all over as soon as Ovett raised the pace
around the last bend. It was a race about a loser rather
than a winner. Coe has much to do in the 1,500 metres
to reject the accusation that he is not a man who can
cope with championship racing. His frail frame can be
prepared for that one explosive night in Oslo or Zürich,
where he can run the world off its feet, but in the
demanding cockpit of a championship he is left wanting
both mentally and physically, on this evidence. The last
time he came on this parade was in the European
Championships two years ago, and there he followed
home Ovett when both were beaten. Since then he has
not much bothered with championships, even domestic
ones, and his studied avoidance of Ovett ... has now
come home to roost. It was never less than a well
thought out way of running, but the more simplistic idea
of putting his toe in the bath to see how hot the water is
would have proved a better scheme. The red carpet for
victory was rolled out on Saturday and he did not see it.
Coe, from the outside lane, had the opportunity, and
took it, to avoid the bumping by running wide. No one
wanted to do the front work and the elbows were clash-
ing when the digital clock clicked up a first lap of 54·3.
Ovett was locked in a box with Wagenknecht banging
him in the ribs. It was the moment for Coe to fly; he
would, with his acceleration, have been thirty metres
clear before Ovett could have escaped and that would
have been enough.'

Watman, in spite of his reservations about Ovett's rough
tactics, asserted in *Athletics Weekly*: 'One can state with
some authority that Steve is the greatest big-time competitor ever to wear the British vest.' And in the *Express* I
wrote:

'Ovett crushingly taught Coe the age old Olympic lesson
in Saturday's long awaited 800 metres final – first is

first, second is nowhere. The experienced, gritty racer beat the finely tuned record-breaker in a slow affair which was an anti-climax. Now a huge question mark hangs over Coe. Unless he exacts revenge in Friday's 1,500 metres final, or at least pushes Ovett to a new world record, his prestige will take a hammering. While Ovett is poised to emulate New Zealander Peter Snell's 1964 double in Tokyo, Coe has first to recover from his novice-like defeat.'

From the evidence, I was sure he could.

━━━━━━━━

❬ It was natural for people to ask themselves, 'has the guy got brains?' In fact, I wasn't aware of the extent of the criticism because I deliberately hadn't read a single newspaper all the time I was in the Village. But I did sit down and wonder whether it was a one-off blunder, whether I did have the racing intelligence. I mentioned to Peter that maybe in future I should find a few more races where there was some messing about in the early stages. How can a silver medal mean nothing? At the kind of level Steve and I had lived at, the life-style we'd adopted, you don't regard a silver medal as acceptable. You don't totally reorganize your life for a year, relinquishing friends and normal contacts, with a view to winning the silver. Even Steve admitted to me, 'I don't know sometimes if it's worth it'. Eamonn Coghlan knew how I felt, he told me, 'I was the fastest finisher in the 1,500 metres in Montreal and threw it away, there was a wall in front and I was boxed, I should have had a medal.' I'm willing to accept, in retrospect, that the magnitude of the Games may have got to me, the pressure did undermine me. ❭

━━━━━━━━

The pressure did not lessen, it intensified. Not only did Seb realize that his reputation with the public and his status within athletics depended upon a convincing display

on Friday, but he had become aware of a planned TV
coup which would centre upon Ovett if he now achieved
the double. There was a move, according to reliable
sources, to promote a series of world-wide invitation meetings packaged around Ovett. If Seb lost, it was probable
that he would be frozen out of the series, which would be
designed to launch Ovett to a new clutch of world records.
Ovett had already claimed in a Sunday newspaper, the day
after his gold medal in the 800 metres, that he and Seb
were 'worth millions in promotional terms'. But Seb was
against both a professional circus, and also the concept of
a TV spectacular staged under existing 'amateur' regulations . . . without him! The only way to torpedo the plan
was to win the 1,500 metres.

   He was also now put under additional pressure, inadver-
tently, by Peter. From the experience of his ten-mile
morning run, Seb sensed that it would be best to keep out
of the way of the press for a while. But Peter, passing the
time mid-morning as usual at the open-air café of the
international area of the Village, gave an interview to the
daily paper correspondents, which was published on the
Monday. In it he repeated, being the direct man he is, the
opinion he had expressed to Seb: that he had 'run like an
idiot'. He also talked of humiliation.

   Words such as 'idiot' and 'humiliation' are the twenty
pound notes of journalistic currency. The reporter confronted by them in an interview would be failing in his
trade if he did not use them in the controversial circumstances of such an Olympic upset. It is not the job of the
writer to protect the speaker from his own indiscretions.
Many reporters, already disposed to be critical of either
the runner or his coach or both after such a gaffe, now
also discovered, as they thought, the coach putting the
boot in about his son. Theirs was not to reason why.
Peter's words were splashed liberally over Monday's
breakfast tables.

   By Tuesday lunchtime the impact at home of father
slamming son had been beamed back to the Village. Seb
confronted Peter in something of a quandary. He was
annoyed at his father's indiscretion, yet still carried a

sense of guilt that he *had* badly let down the man who had given him such devotion, emotional and practical. Peter explained his actions, saying: 'Under no circumstances was I going to let the press think it was the *real* you out there. It wasn't bad luck, you weren't beaten, you *lost* it. The more people who realized that the better.'

⸻

❝I wouldn't have minded if Peter had said it was humiliating for *him*. It was. People were entitled to ask what kind of advice he'd been giving me, but on balance I was less annoyed with Peter's public comments than about some of the press comment on him. To have Hugh McIlvanney of *The Observer* say that Peter 'shadowed me everywhere' I found insulting. If I'd known at the time, instead of when I got back to England, I'd have been furious. What right had he to make such assumptions about my father, how much had he really seen us working together? For a long time I had put up with the uninformed comment that Peter's coaching was something to boost his own ego. Enormously strong ties are developed between athlete and coach, and people were entitled to criticize my running, or Peter's coaching, but *not* our relationship after only the most casual observation.

It was an embarrassing few days with the press whenever I met any of them in the Village. Many of them were avoiding my eye because *they* were embarrassed. They'd say, 'well, there's still Friday, you can do it,' but their manner and their eyes told me they didn't believe it. Not that I hold that against any of them, why should they have thought otherwise? Colin Hart saw me and said good humouredly, 'I'm not going to say anything, but you'd better bloody well do it next time!' And Benny Hill of the *Sheffield Morning Telegraph* said to me when I got home, 'you set them all up, what else could they write?' But it did get under my skin a bit, that so many of the press were emphatic that I wasn't a racer, that they seemed to overlook the way I won the Europa Cup, that they

wouldn't allow me that one horrible mistake. I suppose it
was the fact that it came on top of Prague.

Yet from the moment I had that run on Sunday morning I felt I was on the path to recovery. I had lunch and
went down to the stadium to watch the final of the 10,000
metres. The photographers seemed as intent on me as on
the race, constantly turning to point their telescopic 'mis-
sile launchers' at me in the stand. It was a great race, Yifter winning after such a brave bid by Viren, and it did me
good to get back to the atmosphere of the track. Perhaps
I'd isolated myself too much before the 800 metres. When
I came out from the stadium I met Ron Pickering from
BBC TV, who said, 'people are wondering if we've got
any friends left'. Steve had just given his exclusive interview with Metcalfe for ITV, and this had left the BBC
standing at the post a bit. I agreed to do an interview for
them with Harry Carpenter, but it made me feel that I
was having to carry not only myself, but people in the
media. One got the impression that the competition between the two channels was as important as the Games!'

＝＝＝＝＝

On Tuesday, the day before the 1,500 metres heats, Seb
received a letter from Chris Brasher in which he had out-
lined opinions on how Seb should run the 1,500 metres,
following discussions he had had with Australian former
multi world-record holder Ron Clarke. The sentiments of
Brasher and Clarke were admirable: the race plan they had
devised for Seb less certain. Brasher wrote:

> 'Your own talent has given you the chance to emerge as
> *the* champion of these games. As Ron says, you have to
> take your chance when it is there, and he missed his in
> the 5,000 metres in Tokyo. No pace can drop you off,
> and you are also the fastest in the field, and that is an
> unbeatable combination. The only person who can beat
> you is yourself. Because you cannot be dropped and you
> are also the fastest, you are the Hunter. You can dictate
> the race. Ron thinks you are still the best, but now a lot

of people think the other bloke is. All it needs is an iron determination in your heart. Get that into your mind and then, in the race, relax, move up, and strike.'

In between this fundamental and encouraging advice were elaborate instructions on the tactics which Seb should employ against either Bayi or Ovett or both. While the encouragement was the sincere contribution of two former world-class runners to another, the tactical recommendations rather presumed an absence of discussions between Seb and his father!

———

‘It was kind of Chris to take the trouble, and I was grateful for the gesture, for the knowledge that two men such as they should consider I was unbeatable if I ran it the right way – though their way was not quite the same as mine, and in the event Bayi withdrew to concentrate on the 3,000 metres steeplechase. He was determined to win Tanzania's first ever medal in the Games, he wanted that more than any personal glory and in the end he got the silver, after a dramatic race in which he led by almost fifty metres with three laps to go and was finally caught by Malinowski. It was on the Tuesday, the same day as I received Brasher's letter, that Brendan started his psychotherapy, threatening me with the idea that if I lost again there would be only one runner in Britain who mattered, that if I lost again the critics would be bracketing me with Dave Bedford, a record breaker who had flopped in the Munich Olympics and the Christchurch Commonwealth Games. 'Do you want that?'

I felt I was now getting back into a state of aggression, partly through anger at my own performance, partly because everyone was writing me off so quickly. It would be all very well for David Coleman to say after the 1,500 metres 'you don't become a bad athlete overnight', but that hadn't always been his view during the previous week. The Wednesday of the first round of the 1,500 metres was the hottest day of the Games yet, but the

heats on the whole were unexceptional. In mine, I went to
the front and stayed there, and ran down the final straight
together with Fontanella of Italy, with him looking side-
ways at me most of the way. After the race I went back
into the stadium to watch the rest of the day with Peter.
He was slightly annoyed that I'd not won, Fontanella had
got the verdict by inches in the identical time of 3:40·1.
Peter had said, 'go out and run like a world record holder
and cleanse yourself'. He was beginning to be quite severe
with me. We went back to the Village and had a large
meal, cooked meat, potatoes, sweet-corn, and two pints of
orange juice – the middle distance runner's diet. Then a
massage back in the British quarters, and bed. **'**

With the first four in each heat and the two fastest losers
to qualify for the semi-finals, Steve Cram had to work
hard at the finish in the first heat, won by Marajo, to get
in front of the Russian Yakoylev for fourth place. Ovett
took the fourth heat a stride ahead of Jurgen Straub of
East Germany in 3:36·8. The draw for the two semis kept
Ovett and Coe apart, and Ovett clearly had the harder
prospect. His draw included Malozemlin, the fancied Russian, Busse, Cram, Zdravkovic, and Loikanen of Finland.
Seb's only serious challenger was Straub. In the event it
was Seb who had to run the faster to be first home – after
a considerable scare before the race.

'I had a good ten hours' sleep after the heats, and
had two miles of easy jogging early in the morning. I
somehow felt it would be the hardest of the two semi-
finals, and I was pleased it was going to be late in the
evening, after nine, which is when I'm at my best. I
wanted to win well, a full dress rehearsal for the following
day. I was walking back to the Village after lunch when
suddenly I had stomach pains. I'd got the bug which had
K.O.'d Dave Moorcroft! I immediately got tablets from

the team doctor to close me up, thinking, 'this is all I need!'. I didn't panic, I went to bed and slept. The tablets worked, sealed me up, but I felt uncomfortable inside, carrying all that rubbish.

Apart from needing physiotherapy to keep my hamstring flexible, my physical state was improving all the time. I travelled down to the stadium for the semis with Steve and Harry, we had a car booked and offered them and Steve Cram a lift and arranged a time to collect them afterwards, but when it came they didn't turn up. I was in the second race, and the tone was set in the first few strides when Tischenko, the Russian, cut across from the outside. I remember handing him off and moving to the front, in behind Straub, who led for the first two laps. Down the back straight for the third time I surged to keep pace with Nemeth of Austria as he came through, and I handed off Straub as he tried to come with us. At the bell I was just behind Nemeth, followed by Straub and Marajo. On the last bend I stupidly allowed Fontanella and Marajo to go past me on the outside, temporarily boxing me in, and I had to produce a really fierce burst to get clear again. I was aware I had made a mistake, but not how glaring it was till I caught Peter's eye after the race. His expression said, 'what are you trying to do to me?' For three days he'd been drumming into me: 'Be in touch with the leader, no more than a stride down going into the last bend, and run wide almost into the second lane, so that if anybody tries to go past they have to run really wide, and you still have the space to respond and go past the leader if you need to.'❜

═══════════

Up in the stand Brasher and Clarke looked at each other and agreed: 'He's had it. He hasn't got a tactical brain.' It had certainly been a blunder, but the acceleration with which Seb corrected it was one of the most electric of any race in the Games. He crossed the line a fraction ahead of Straub in 3:39·4, almost four seconds faster than Ovett's winning time in the first semi. Cram, in a desperate finish

with Malozemlin in which both were given the same time
of 3:43·6, had just squeezed fourth place to qualify for the
final at the age of nineteen. Plachy of Czechoslovakia,
fifth in Coe's semi, was the fastest 'loser' to make up the
nine in the final. They would be:

	Qualifying time	Personal best
Jurgen Straub (GDR)	3:39·4	3:33·7
Jose Marajo (France)	3:39·6	3:35·1
Andreas Busse (GDR)	3:43·5	3:37·1
Steve Cram (GB)	3:43·6	3:35·6
Vittorio Fontanella (Italy)	3:40·1	3:38·3
Sebastian Coe (GB)	3:39·4	3:32·1
Jozef Plachy (Czechoslovakia)	3:40·4	3:37·2
Steve Ovett (GB)	3:43·1	3:32·1
Dragan Zdravkovic (Yugoslavia)	3:43·4	3:38·0

‹I suppose you could say my 1,500 metres semi-
final wasn't any better than the 800 metres final as a
bargeing match. I felt ashamed about it, even more so
when people came up afterwards and said, 'that's the
way, we knew you were on the way back when you started
throwing them out of your path!' I had to play down being
boxed in, especially when I saw Peter's face. As we sat by
the warm-up track afterwards Peter was saying, 'if you do
that tomorrow, you're dead.' I did six or seven laps to
warm down in the dark, I didn't want to leave the junk in
my legs from a fairly fast race. It was late before we had
dinner and I finally got to bed. But I slept very well.
Instead of the nerves I had before the 800 metres, I was
now excited by the final of the 1,500 metres, I wanted to
get out there and enjoy it.›

Peter and I leaned on the railing of the warm-up track as
Seb floated round, disappearing into the darkness on the

far side and then reappearing into the finishing straight, illuminated dimly by a few bulbs along the front of the small changing pavilion. Two other shadowy figures were warming down: Seb's German rivals Straub and Busse, observed by a posse of coaches. Peter looked tired and drawn. He had been troubled by a bad ankle, from the miles of walking one had to do around the Village and the stadium and the hotels. He was sixty, and the pressure was getting at him, too. The tension was if anything worse for him than for his son because, as with any coach, once any race began, he was powerless to affect the outcome. As we stared out now into the darkness, he was no longer planning, just day-dreaming about what he knew was possible but at that moment was still far off. 'At least his stomach held out', he said to me without turning his head, knowing that Seb's stomach was the least of the problems. The weak electric light accentuated the lines in Peter's thin face; like his son he'd come a long way, at a time of life when the effort was going to show. He said: 'If he only does what he's capable of, there is no one tomorrow who will touch him. Not just because it's painful, but I'd give my right arm for him to go to the line again tomorrow in the same frame of mind as he did for the Oslo Mile last year. *That* was my runner.' Seb came off the track smiling and relaxed. Maybe he would go to the line 'all together'.

Brasher and Clarke were not alone, even if in a minority, in believing that the gun would go with Seb the logical favourite. Cliff Temple had written after the 800 metres final: 'Last night's result may have only a marginal effect on the 1,500 metres. The demands are slightly different: four years ago John Walker of New Zealand was eliminated in his 800 metres heat but he still went on to win the 1,500 metres final. Friday's race is still the big showdown.' After the evening's two semi-finals I had cabled to the *Express*: 'If Sebastian Coe is within striking distance of Steve Ovett 200 metres from the finish of today's classic Olympic 1,500 metres final, he will win.'

In all his races thus far Ovett had been sign-writing in the air with his right hand after he crossed the line: a message, which was said to be I.L.Y. for 'I Love You', aimed at the television cameras for the benefit of his girlfriend back home. As this supreme runner had entered the final straight of his semi-final, he had waved cheerily to his mother in the crowd. I sensed he was taunting destiny.

8: Release

Early on the day of the final, under yet another cloudless blue sky, I made the ten mile journey out to the Village and there, on a grassy bank, I found Kenny Moore, US marathon runner and writer for *Sports Illustrated*, looking rather forlorn in singlet and tracksuit bottom and his inevitable training shoes. 'Every time I ring my office and talk to them, they say "fine, Kenny, but you've only got half of the story". They're convinced Ovett is going to win again, it's *the* event of the whole Games back in the States, and I need to get hold of Steve, but I can never find the fellow.' Kenny, a personal friend of the Coes, had the look of a man who has an important plane to catch and is convinced he is going to miss it. Was even he now doubting Seb, I thought to myself? His doubt would have been magnified had he known the extent of the trouble from Seb's sciatic-related hamstring.

⟨It was vital that I was able to get a really good massage twice a day. Helen Bristow, the physio who looked after me, did an exceptional job, she worked very hard to keep the tendon loose. It showed her integrity, too, she never spoke a word to anyone, not even to her several friends among the press, whom she had known for a number of

years. The news would have aroused the press enormously; but if I'd let it be known at the time and then lost
again, it would have been said it was sour grapes. The
work of all the physios, who were on duty from dawn till
midnight and hardly ever had the chance even to leave the
Village, could not have been more selfless and pains-
taking. They gave us psychotherapy as much as
physiotherapy. Allan Wells was convinced at one stage
that he had torn muscle fibres, when in fact he'd only had
cramp in the middle of the night. They cured him and
calmed him down.

Everyone out there on the administrative side did a
marvellous job, too. The team managers Nick Whitehead,
Lynn Davies, and Mary Peters didn't miss a trick. It was a
colossal improvement on the old days, having people who
were *for* the athletes and not for themselves. They were
working an eighteen-hour day, right down to getting the
draws off the computer at midnight for the next day's
events, so that when we got up next morning we would
know what the programme was. They were good people to
be with, former top-line athletes who knew the pressures
and the priorities.

Nick, to use an old fashioned description, is an absolute
gent, you never hear him raise his voice, while Lynn's
big-time experience and Welsh humour were invaluable.
Athletes don't need motivating at an Olympics, they need
all irritations in their paths smoothed out for them, an
understanding of idiosyncrasies, an acceptance that we are
all different. Mary, too, was all these things, tremendously
caring and emotional. At one stage Russian officials tried
to stop Linsey McDonald from going out for the 4 × 400
metres relay medal ceremony because she had the wrong
tracksuit bottom, and Mary rushed round to find something – far too large – which little Linsey had to roll up
five times, but it got her out there.

I had the usual early-morning run before the final, my
stomach had cleared and the problem was now out of my
mind. I sensed the Village was beginning to buzz about
the race, that not many people thought I could do it but
they wanted to be there. I'd heard what the bookies' odds

were at home. When I was told they were 11 to 4 on Steve I smiled, it could have been something out of *The Sting*, as if I had deliberately thrown the 800 metres, in order to shift a pile on to the 1,500 metres! How could the odds be that short on a two-horse race? George had sent me a telegram after the 800 metres: 'The bookies have retired, now for your Number One event.' If a knowledgeable critic such as Rodda says I'm not going to win, that's fair enough, but I felt the bookies' odds were ridiculous. It acted as an additional spur. ❯

───────

I met Seb after an early lunch and wandered down to the almost deserted training track on the fringe of the Village. The only other person there was a large, hirsute Bulgarian swimmer in a bikini. Brendan had delivered his last pep-talk to Seb: 'Win this, and you can go on to take the lot in the future, the 5,000 metres and even the 10,000 metres. The other guy can win it, of course, but you can go out there and piss it. There's no way he can do that. But lose it, and you could be finished.' We were sitting on white plastic chairs under a sunshade. Seb was so at ease we could have been back home in the garden. I slipped him a succession of casual, conversational questions about his condition, his conviction, his tactics. I asked him if there was any single aspect of the race that he feared. The answers, though equally casual, were unhesitating. I knew then he was ready for probably the most important race he would ever have to run.

More than at any time in the past week he was at one with himself. For months I had observed the Himalayan effort, dedication and self-denial which had gone into preparing for this moment. I knew the extent of his self-motivation, and now he was convinced that he could do to his great rival what Ovett had so unerringly done to others for the last three years: stay close to the pace-maker, in touch whatever the speed, and strike on the final bend. I said to him that a few minutes of physical or mental pain this afternoon would be worth the endur-

ing glory. He looked up and simply said: 'Why not?' Peter
arrived and joined us. He re-emphasized that if Seb stayed
with the pace right at the front, the only way he could lose
was by being boxed. His last, pragmatic instruction was, 'if
necessary – punch!'

━━━━━━━

    ‘I was well aware that there was more pressure on
me in this race than in any I had ever run, but I felt good.
As we walked through the security exit gate of the Village, the inevitable hand-held camera crews homed in, the
luckless interviewers going through the boring routine
questions – How do you see it? Interesting. Are you confident? Yes. Can you win it? Yes. Have you seen Steve
today? No. The same old stuff. I wondered how they
would ever get it back to London before the race was
already over. Even our Russian car driver, who took us
down to the stadium, was more switched on than usual,
enquiring in broken English: 'Ovut good. You vin?'
grinning and showing his gold fillings. It wasn't like the 800
metres: I was alive, I just wanted to get down there and get
on with it, get finished with Moscow and the Games as soon
as I could.’

━━━━━━━

After I left Seb at the training track, I met David Shaw
outside the Village and we jumped into a taxi to head
back to the Rossiya where he was also based, for a change
of clothes in the sweltering heat before setting off for the
stadium and the climax of the Games, including the
marathon. As we crossed the Moscva River and headed
for the centre of the city, we ran into chaos. The Russians,
reacting as in so many instances with over-efficiency, had
closed all roads approaching the river-bank marathon
course about two hours before it was necessary, with the
result that even Moscow's moderately congested traffic
was already paralyzed and at a horn-blowing, fist-waving,
radiator-boiling standstill. Even though our cab driver rose

to the occasion with a burst of improvization which broke every rule in the police manual, he was stumped. We tried every back double, failed abysmally to bribe our way through police road blocks with official British team lapel badges, and even though going the wrong way down several one-way-streets were finally forced to abandon the taxi and run the last half mile to the Rossiya. David Shaw immediately telephoned the Village to make sure that British competitors allowed themselves plenty of time to get down to the stadium.

———

❝I knew the aggression which had been lacking in the 800 metres was back for the 1,500 metres when I used appalling language to two guards, who tried to cut off the approach to the warm-up track because of the marathon, which had just begun. When we got out on to the track in the Lenin Stadium after the warm up, the British supporters had built up a tremendous noise, chanting the names of Steve and me. This race was for them. I don't remember too much of the preliminaries, my mental cut-out following the warm up was this time working properly. Steve and I and young Steve Cram all wished each other luck. Ovett said to me, 'give it stick' in a friendly way, and suggested we should have a drink together after the race. He seemed confident.❞

———

The sun beat down. The tension was electric. Our first glimpse of the runners was in their tracksuits among the guards at the entrance to the tunnel. Zdravkovic was the first to appear, then the powerfully muscled Straub, then Seb in a grey top, followed by Ovett, frowning as he came out into the sunlight. Suddenly the order was given and like a pack of foxhounds they broke away down the back straight for the final, statutory warm up. Seb did several stooping exercises to stretch his hamstring, then turned in front of the huge contingent of East German supporters at

the end of the back straight, and ran back side by side
with Ovett towards the tunnel. As they went, they passed
the Nero-like figure of Andy Norman, standing alone in
shirt sleeves with arms folded, down in one of the photographers' dug-outs. At last the nine finalists, stripped and
sleek, were led single file towards the start, now on an
invisible leash. They lined up, jostled, regrouped – and the
gun went. Straub and Seb went straight to the front, with
the blond Plachy at the back of the group.

    ❪ It was a pedestrian pace but there was very little
bargeing for such a slow procession. Jurgen ran just ahead
of me, always with his head down as if he were looking
for marks on the track, but he was locked into his own private world, he knew what he had come to do. I was very
relaxed, completely free of worry, though others may have
thought that I was once more playing into Steve's hands. ❫

As they came off the first bend into the home straight they
were grouped in twos: Straub and Coe, Marajo and Ovett,
Cram and Busse, Fontanella and Zdravkovic. On they
went, cautious, contained. Down the second back straight
Cram had moved up alongside Ovett, ahead of Marajo.
Other than that, there was no change as the pack, still
unbroken, moved sedately to the 800 metres mark in
2:4·9. It was now that Straub made the move which would
convert the race from a stroll into a remorseless burn all
the way to the tape.

    ❪ Suddenly I realized Straub was going for broke, I
knew that no one could take over that kind of pace, not
that they would not want to. I had to follow Jurgen, and I
guessed instinctively that Steve would be tracking me so as

to have both of us in his sights. He would know that I was
the one to follow, that Jurgen had sacrificed his final kick by
making his bid so far from home. When Jurgen went, he
opened up daylight and I had to fasten on very quick –
and it just kept getting quicker. I felt comfortable. Suddenly it was single file, and I was running free in a lane
of my own. I knew that sustained speed of this sort would
play into my hands. I'd always been confident, arrogant if
you like, that I could maintain that speed longer than
anyone. I was out on the Rivelin Valley Road again, but
this time it was Jurgen's back ahead of me and not my
father's car. *And* I was in a position to break first.**'**

———

From the dawdle of the first two laps, 61·6 for the first
followed by 63·3, Jurgen Straub had lifted the third to a
searing 54·6. Up in the stands, Peter was convinced the
race was as good as over. 'No one in the world can keep
that speed the way Seb can. It didn't look fast, because
the front three were all such superb stylists.' At the bell,
the order had been, strung out in line: Straub, Coe, Ovett,
Busse, Fontanella, Marajo, with Cram trying to hold on in
seventh position. Into the back straight for the last time
the order remained the same. Ovett, the television com-
mentators were saying as if in unison, was poised for victory.

———

' At the 1,200 metres mark, Straub dug his head
down again for a final assault and I had to respond. Going
into the final bend I was right on his shoulder. Down the
back straight I'd been conscious that we were coming to
the physical climax of the race, that I was going to have to
give it everything. I knew that the previous 600 metres would
have softened everyone behind. We were into an area
where we were no longer middle distance runners, where
the hours of conditioning in training were needed: 'sprint,

drive, work the arms'. I put in a semi-kick at 180 metres, and that carried me past Jurgen, there was daylight and I could hear his feet receding. **'**

What Seb did not know was that his kick had almost exactly coincided with Ovett's bid to overtake *him*, and now Ovett saw the gap between them stretch to another stride and a half. The 'split' times would show that Seb was actually accelerating the whole way from 180 metres to 50 metres out.

'I put in another semi-kick coming off the bend and took two glances back down either side. Jurgen was still just in vision inside, with Steve right in line behind him so that I couldn't see him. I was now running for the tape, the mental agony of knowing I had hit my limit, of not knowing what was happening back there behind me. I was not to know they were fading too. I tried to drive again at 40 metres out, and in the next few strides I knew I had nothing left if anyone came back at me. The anxiety over the last 20 metres was unbearable, and it showed in my face as I crossed the line. After a few yards I sank down onto my knees. When I watched that display on the replay it was a bit embarrassing, but it was such a bloody marvellous relief. **'**

Seb had won the gold medal with a last 800 metres of 1:48·5, the fastest last two laps ever run in a three-and-a-half or four-lap race. The last 300 metres had been covered in 39, the last 200 metres in 24.7, the last 100 metres in 12·1! His winning time of 3:38·4 might be over six seconds outside his world record, but who cared?

On a street in the middle of Liverpool Seb's closest friend at Loughborough, Sean Butler, a middle distance man who had shared countless long hours grinding out the miles on the road in winter, and whose gentle wit and relaxed nature had contributed much towards maintaining a normal balance in his companion's pressurized life, was watching the race in the window of a TV retailer. He was one of a large crowd which had gathered, and at the end of the first lap he had exclaimed, 'Christ, Ovett looks good'. Thereafter he had managed to keep his thoughts to himself, even when that final glorious run for home began. In the hubbub on the pavement after the finish, another Liverpudlian turned to Sean and said: 'I don't know what you're smiling about. You wanted Ovett to win!'

⸻

‹I remember going off on my lap of honour and having to side step the blazer brigade. I'd won – and I flipped. I didn't know what I was doing. I couldn't believe it would feel the way it did. It wouldn't have been half as good, as acute, if I hadn't gone through the previous few days. They were dreadful days. I'd bottled it all up, and now the emotion was coming out like champagne that had been shaken. I put my arm round Steve, but it was all reflex. As I ran down the back straight, the one great overriding feeling was that I was free, 'I don't need this hassle any more, I don't have to put up with the aggro if I don't want to'. To have that kind of feeling so soon, a psychologist might say that I had actually lost some of the joy of running, and for a short while I would probably have agreed. I just hadn't realized the extent of the pressure. Yet thirty minutes later I was in the press conference and talking about moving up to the 5,000 metres in 1984. I knew I could now retire at any point and feel a satisfied man. Not that I'd achieved everything which was possible, far from it, there were more world records to break, more gold medals to win, but could they ever mean as much? It had never been my intention to go on racing indefinitely.›

The praise now heaped upon Seb exceeded even the criticism of the previous week. Ian Wooldridge wrote on the front page of the *Daily Mail*:

'Coe did more than win the gold medal. He lifted the soul, he ennobled his art, he dignified his country . . . Watching him run, invincible, over the last 300 metres was unforgettable. Watching him afterwards made you even prouder, for his conduct in triumph matched his humility in disaster . . . He wasn't here to settle some parochial feud by incinerating Steve Ovett. For six days he had had to live with himself for running so far below his intellect in the 800 metres and losing to Ovett that his only challenger yesterday was himself.'

In *The Times* Norman Fox reported:

'Once bitten, but not twice shy . . . it was pride as much as medals and records that were at issue and this time Coe refused to be driven into awkward situations in the longer, more studied race. This was Ovett's first defeat in forty-six races. There was no question that it was done without room for further debate, and at the end he accepted it with the grace that some people doubted was in his soul.'

Peter Hildreth who, in the previous week's *Sunday Telegraph* had stated that Coe had no chance on earth, now called it 'a sublime finale' and added:

'Coe was timed over the last 800 metres in 1:48·9 – fast enough to earn a passage for several runners through the heats of the 800 metres. It was treatment like this meted out by Pekka Vasala of Finland which proved the undoing of the great Kip Keino in the Munich 1,500 metres final in 1972. It was also too much for Ovett. Though the flowing rhythm was held, Ovett had no upper register when Coe made his move off the final turn. And Coe's winning two-stage kick was no ad lib invention.'

Filbert Bayi and Seb in Oslo—potential Moscow rivals. In the event Bayi withdrew from the 1,500m to concentrate on the steeplechase, taking the silver medal

Seb beats Willi Wulbeck in the 1,000m in Oslo in a world record of 2:13.40—to hold a unique quartet. But an hour later Steve Ovett took the mile

(*Popperfoto*)

ela Domokos)

'No, I didn't know Ovett thinks he has a 90 per cent chance in the 1,500m!'
Seb diplomatically handles a 400-strong international press conference on his
second day in Moscow

(Popperfoto)

Father and son in earnest discussion in the Olympic Village prior to the ill-fated 800m final

**The 800m medal ceremony: Coe (silver), Ovett (gold),
and Nikolai Kirov of Russia (bronze)**

(The Associated Press Ltd)

(*The Associated Press L*)

Vainly Seb tries to make up the lost ground on his arch rival, Steve Ovett, as they battle towards the tape with East German Detlef Wagenknecht (fifth) at the end of the 800m

(Opposite) Four phases on the way to the 1,500m gold medal. Top: at 200m Straub (338) has the lead, which he held for three-quarters of the race. Behind, on the inside, is Cram (257); Coe (254) is running wide and obscures Marajo (243), with Ovett (279) obscuring Plachy (783) and Fontanella (426), and Busse (296) running wide beside Ovett. Top centre: at 600m the three Britons are relaxed, behind Straub, with Zdravkovic (767) bringing-up the rear of the nine-man field. Bottom centre: at 1,000m Straub suddenly begins his long burst for home and Coe and Ovett respond instantly. Bottom: into the final straight, at 1,400m, Coe makes his second 'kick' to take Straub, leaving Ovett and Busse (obscured) two and three strides adrift

200 metres

600 metres

1,000 metres

1,400 metres

(*The Associated Press Ltd*)

The agony and the ecstacy at the finish of 'the race of the century'—the picture which was spread across the front page of over 800 newspapers around the world

(Left below) Seb sinks to his knees in a mixture of relief and satisfaction

(Below) Having conquered his nerves in a six-day battle, the jubilant victor sets off on a lap of honour

(Syndication International Ltd)

A different sort of police escort from that in Moscow as the champion arrives back at London Airport

Three Brits in Zurich: Seb, Daley Thompson and Allan Wells receive acclaim for their gold medals from the Swiss crowd. Seb later failed by a fraction of a second to lower his 1,500m record

(Bela Domokos)

‘When I finally ran off the track after the lap of honour, I accidently ran hard into Ron Pickering, there with a microphone, and almost knocked him over. 'How does it feel?' he asked. All I could reply was, 'Oh, Christ', which subsequently earned me a sharp reprimand from the Bishop of Durham. In the background Mike Murphy was saying, 'bloody magic, bloody magic'. As we waited in the dope-testing room, we were asked by a Russian official if we would attend the press conference. Straub and I said yes, Steve said no, and added, 'I'm surprised you're going, after the stick you've been given these last five days'. I laughed and truthfully said I hadn't seen it, though I knew about it; I was surprised that the guy who was supposed to be indifferent to the press was in fact so sensitive. As we stood around waiting for the doping formalities – 'are these your two samples, sign the labels please, initial the corks please' – Steve said to me, 'it takes a bit of time to sink in doesn't it?' I replied, 'well, we've both been losers out here, and we've both sacrificed a lot in our lives to be winners'. After a while Steve said, 'I don't know, do you think the sacrifice is worth all this. I begin to wonder.' I just wondered if he would have said that if he'd won. Yet there's a streak in me which was glad he didn't go back home with nothing, because I knew exactly how I would have felt.

The rest of the evening was chaos, one endless succession of television studios. Brasher leaped into a car with us to go to the television studios the other side of Moscow, to complete his story for Sunday. ITV arranged a link-up with my mother in the YTV studio in Leeds, but it got delayed while Peter and John Walker, who was in the London studio with Dickie Davies, became involved in a four-minute discussion on tactics, until Davies finally said, 'you must be waiting to speak to your wife'. My mother looked a trifle smashed, and was certainly very happy! When Peter said goodbye he added, 'and go carefully on my Scotch', absolutely dead-pan. Probably half the population back home thought he was serious: he'd had a go at his son, now it was his wife! As we left the studios, approaching midnight, Brasher said that he was going to be running in the New York marathon. I told him my letter would be in the post.**❜**

━━━━━━━

More than twenty million people in Britain had watched that hypnotic three-and-a-half minute race on TV – stopping work in the office or factory, standing in the street to watch in retailers' windows, even taking the afternoon off. They were drawn by the magnetism of one slim young runner and his race with himself, as much as with his brilliant arch-rival. Derek Johnson, 1956 silver medallist at 800 metres and Chairman of the International Athletic Club, summed up succinctly: 'It was the greatest finish to a 1,500 metres since Jack Lovelock's in 1936. To kick twice at that pace was something I had not believed possible.' When Seb arrived home, such was the crush of well-wishers and press and photographers at London Airport that police sealed off the M4 system for several minutes to permit him to show a clean pair of heels for the second time in three days.

9: Freedom

Leni Riefenstahl's film of the Nazi Olympics in Berlin in 1936 exposed all their prophetic military overtones. What we saw in the closing ceremony of the 1980 Olympic Games in Moscow was equally ominous. It may be that the western world, for all its current misgivings, is not as vulnerable to a power bid from a nation with acute internal political and economic problems as Europe was in 1935–9, but there was no mistaking the message of Soviet might which was relayed to the world at that ceremony. The mood may have been lightened with decorative folk dancing, but the massive exhibition of synchronized gymnastic efficiency was symbolic of the domination of the individual by the state. And the three supreme leaders of the armed forces, whose images were interwoven into the display, possessed three of the hardest faces I think I have ever seen. It was with a shudder, not a song, that I left the stadium with Peter at the conclusion.

Seb has stated with clarity his reasons for believing that the British did right to oppose the boycott advocated by the government. I find myself in an ambivalent position, believing on the one hand that the boycott was morally right, but that the government forfeited their case, and swung the majority of the population against them, by presenting it so clumsily and insincerely. There is probably little disparity between my standpoint and Seb's, and I

147

think my post-Olympic attitude was perfectly stated in the following leader in *The Times*:

'There were several ideas behind the attempt to boycott the Moscow Olympics. The main one was that the Soviet Union should be denied the propaganda advantage which it hoped to reap from the Games. In many statements the Soviet Union had made it clear that the Games were to be presented not only as a sort of coming-out party at which the world, by attending, would be recognizing the success and respectability of the Soviet Union, but also as a specific endorsement of Soviet "peace policy" abroad. In other words the Games were to be a highly political event designed to further Soviet policies and win support for them.

'This was, of course, true from the moment the Games were awarded to Moscow, but at that time many felt that the propaganda advantage to the Soviet Union would be outweighed by the benefits of diminishing the isolation which contributes to some of the less desirable aspects of Soviet policy. After Afghanistan, the balance swung the other way. It was rightly felt that to grant the Soviet Union a specific endorsement of its foreign policy while it was killing people in occupied Afghanistan would be morally abhorrent and politically unwise. The fact that the boycott was, in the end, patchy in its execution and limited in its effects does not mean that the attempt was wrong or not worthwhile. To have tried and partly failed is much better than not to have tried at all. In only one respect does the partial boycott seem to have been a total failure. As far as can be ascertained, the broad masses of the Soviet people got the wrong message or none at all. Most seem to believe that Soviet forces are in Afghanistan to help. They attribute the boycott to American ill-will, and if they are angry it is not at Mr Brezhnev but at Mr Carter. This is a pity but it does not invalidate the attempt.'

‘As I have stated earlier, I think it was necessary for the British to insist on their participation in the Games in order to ensure that international sport should not be wrecked for all time, and should not become fair game for any politicians looking for a platform. Having made my own decision to go, it is impossible for me to say with hindsight how I might have felt if I'd lost both races. Maybe my mother was near the mark when she asked after the 800 metres if I was thinking of retiring. Certainly my career would have been at the cross-roads, yet I like to think that the same thing which churned me up, made me get off my backside and win the 1,500 metres, would have reacted again if I'd lost that. But at what level? Besides, I still consider even now that the Olympics are *not* necessarily a true test of ability. If I'd gone there only for the 800 metres, would the result have meant that I was second best in the world and in Britain? I don't honestly think so. I was often asked before the Games whether I would swop my world record for an Olympic gold medal. I found it difficult to answer. I think the records of 1979 were in fact the truer indication of athletic ability and that's why it's my intention to get them all back at the earliest possible opportunity.’

During the winter of 1980–1 Seb has been preparing for just that, re-aligning his training towards quality rather than the stamina-producing work of the winter of 1979–80, which was geared to the endurance of six races in twelve days in Moscow. During this last winter he has once again become a part-time athlete, concentrating at the same time on his post-graduate course at Loughborough. Yet he finds that under this arrangement his academic life is still compromised.

‘University lecturers and tutors in my first three years considered it insulting if you were not prepared to devote your whole being to their pursuit. I'm not asking for degrees to become mickey-mouse, half-hour oral tests, but universities should provide a student with more than a degree. Under the syllabus at Loughborough I've never fully expanded my mental curiosity. I've cut corners horribly because of athletics. I would have been far happier had I stayed with economic history rather than economics. I was not at ease with the staff, who could only see my outside commitments as devaluing their own purpose. I have found some academics extremely narrow. The day of the rounded man has gone; the British university system is not producing the properly developed, thinking person.

I'm grateful for the added experience athletics has given me even if in some ways it has limited my activities. To an extent it is unnerving to have become public property, it has cut down the number of places I can go to have a normal day out. Unless I go through the turnstiles and stand on the terraces at football matches, there is always the likelihood that I may be asked to make a presentation or something at half-time or after the game, which is perfectly pleasant but you are no longer a private person. I have girlfriends, but mostly no one special – partly because I haven't the time for a close relationship outside the family, but also, with a girl, I have to be so careful that casual remarks are not taken out of context by others. In Sheffield it's almost impossible for me to be seen with a girl, even though she may not even be a personal friend of mine: within hours people are going nudge-nudge, wink-wink all over the place, which can be most unfortunate for the girl as well as for me. Photographers take so many liberties. At one press conference after the 800 metres record, a photographer produced a model girl out of the blue – 'something special, do me a favour', he said – and then when I refused became quite nasty and said, 'have you got girl trouble or something?' **9**

Even his own fans, however well meaning, try to take him over at times. Particularly in the north, there is a feeling that if you become famous then it must be partly due to the fact that you are from the north; that you are part of some gigantic northern freemasonry and that therefore your success belongs not just to you, but to the region. At a Bradford boxing evening where Seb was a guest, he was sitting signing autographs almost continuously from seven till midnight. At one point an elderly man came up to him and, not unfriendly, said, "ere lad, tha's 'ad thi free meal, nah git thi naame dahn on theer', shoving forward a menu. He is 'our' Seb. Passing in the street, a lady remarked to him, 'it's nice to have something in Sheffield that no one else has'. Something. At his second civic reception by the mayor and corporation – the first followed the records, the second was after the Olympics – he spent the better part of two hours graciously saying hello to everyone who mattered, civic, industrial, and union dignitaries, signing autographs and making an impromptu speech, and at the finish he was the *only* person present in the city hall who had not had anything to eat!

When he returned after the Golden Mile in 1979, there was a note waiting from a local athletic organization advising him, in all seriousness, 'if you don't get your entry form in you won't be able to run, we've warned you about this before'. He can be excused for feeling at times that Sheffield is not so much a mother to him as a mother-in-law. Yet his loyalty is strongly to the north: Yorkshire, not Crystal Palace, is his 'home', a fact which people who write even to me complaining if he is absent from a fixture in London do not understand. In 1980 he ran in more domestic events prior to the Games than almost any other Moscow competitor: the Yorkshire championships, the Northern Counties, the Inter-Counties, an international, and the U.K. Closed. And after the Games he cancelled a pre-arranged run in Berlin in order to appear in the Coca-Cola at Crystal Palace. He is patriotic as far as he is able to be where internationals and the Europa Cup are concerned, but critical of discipline among the team when abroad.

⸻

❛The situation has improved considerably with the introduction of team managers who know what they are

doing, there was no comparison, for instance, between
Prague in 1978 and Turin in 1979. But the fact is that
there is still a bit of a folklore hangover about high jinks
on these trips from days gone by. Some members of the
team take the attitude that it is one big carousel. You find
athletes playing dominoes till four in the morning, coming
in late from discos, playing stereo tapes and radios until
all hours, and keeping others awake.

When somebody like Wells or Capes or Foster or me
complains that we're trying to sleep in the afternoon,
that's not being awkward, it's because that's our routine:
not playing frisbee in the corridor. On every trip we go on
there are those who joke about the East Germans or Russians never being seen at the discos, but that's the name of
the game. The ones who denigrate the East German system are the same ones who cannot wait for the next trip
abroad to have a good time, who live their lives vicari-
ously through athletics, and are not prepared to give the
sport what it really needs to succeed. You have to have
discipline, and the sort of enthusiasm which Geoff Capes
has always given. No one has competed in more internationals than Geoff, no one is more patriotic, he's a tremendous team man. He's very outspoken and that's why
he's often been in trouble with the Board, but of all the
present British athletes, he's the one I would be happy to
see as team manager. With him there would be discipline.'

Towards the end of the season a couple of years ago Seb
gave Peter an experimental scare. He had been feeling
lethargic, and as they went off for an evening training stint
he said casually that he had been to the doctor to get a
pick-me-up and that he was 'souped up' for the evening.
Peter went pale, and there was a pause while he considered if Seb was being serious – until his son grinned.

‛Until I was nineteen or twenty I was rather
naïve, I didn't really know what was financially possible in
athletics. Yet now, Daley can say that ultimately he
wants to be a millionaire, and a child can pick up a paper
and read that Ed Moses has received £1,500 for a race in
Italy. So the danger is that if a young athlete discovers
that drugs can be a short-cut to success and material
reward, why should he turn them down? That does not
apply just to world champions, but to club runners wanting to move up from the second team to the first, for
county runners wanting to become internationals. I know
of British athletes who have experimented with drugs,
though I have never been tempted and never would be.
Yet I am low enough down the distance range – towards
the sprint end – for them to be potentially useful. Fortunately I've been able to win without them. But if a coach
said to you that in judicious doses it could do something
startling for you, would you submit? The stupidity is, of
course, that, in the end, you get a situation in which
everyone is on a medical back-up, the difference between
first and third is still going to come down to training and
character, the human factor. I admire Christine Benning,
our leading women's middle distance runner, but I think
she was misguided to take a stand on drugs as a reason for
not going to the Olympics, where she knew the Eastern
Europeans would all be on additives. It would have been
better if she had gone, and had been able to say *she* got
into the last eight *without* taking drugs. That would have
been something to build on. The difference between a
women's 800 metres in 1:53 and 1:55 is probably medical,
but drugs can become a cop-out for British women. I
believe with proper coaching and application there are
British women who could get down to 1:55/1:56. I suspect
that the right distance for Linsey MacDonald is 800
metres, and that if she does not get a medal in 1984 or
1988 it is more likely to be because of factors other than
drugs, factors we all face. Her small size need not necessarily be a limitation at the highest level. At five feet nine
inches and just over nine stone, I was able to break the
world record for 800 metres, yet there is no text book

which says that I ought to be able to do this, and I'm sure
that's why I have been drug tested so often. Linsey
reached an Olympic final at sixteen and there is no reason
why, with careful development, she shouldn't make a very
talented 800 metres runner. I will be disappointed if she
doesn't eventually do something big.*

Twelve days after his gold medal, Seb was back in the
mountains at Macolin in Switzerland, preparing for an
attack on his 1,500 metres world record. The weather was
glorious, and he spent several relaxing days running in the
woods, and we had a superb fish meal down beside Lake
Neuchâtel, watching the surf sailors skimming the water
until the only light was from the hotels and houses wink-
ing along the lakeside. But his hamstring was increasingly
troublesome and needed constant attention. We drove
down to Zürich for the race; Peter and Angela had flown
in that afternoon. Peter passed him the lap times he
thought would do it – 55·5, 1:51·5 (56), 2:48·0 (56·5),
3:30 (42). The field would include Walker, Bayi, Scott,
and Coghlan, with Flynn making the early pace. Would
anyone be able to push him over the third lap as Straub
had done in Moscow?

On a cool evening Flynn took the field through the first
lap ahead of schedule in 54·3, with Seb close on his heels,
followed by the big four. At 800 metres they had slowed
to 1:52·5, a second outside Peter's planned time. Too late
Seb tried to pick up the third lap, and the 1,200 metres
was passed in 2:51·5, three and a half seconds slow.
Although Seb put in a 40·6 last 300 metres, ripping clear
of Walker and Scott around the final turn, he failed by a
fraction, with a time of 3:32·19, to equal the record he
shared with Ovett. It was over six seconds faster than his
winning time in Moscow, the third fastest 1,500 metres
ever run. He was nonetheless disappointed. Even more so
when he arrived home, after losing by inches to Don Paige
in Viareggio, and it was diagnosed that the sciatic trouble
was due to the tilt in his pelvis. He had won the gold

medal running with one leg a quarter of an inch shorter than the other and now he would have to have a complete lay-off, cancelling further planned races in Brussels and Leicester, the latter a mile where he had intended to try to get back that record. He was also a non-starter in the 1980 Golden Mile, this time run at Crystal Palace and won by Ovett with a late burst clear of Scott in 3:52·84. Ovett had failed with a double bid at both 1,500 metres and the mile in Brussels, but running once more at the end of a crowded, eventful season, at Koblenz on 27 August, he improved his and Seb's 1,500 metres record by 0·7 to 3:31·36. The vital factor was that Ovett was taken through the critical third lap in 57·7, for a 1,200 metres time of 2:50·7, by Tom Wessinghage, the West German doctor who had missed the Olympic 5,000 metres because of the boycott, and now ran 3:31·6 himself, also to beat the record.

‹ The greatest reward of the gold medal was that it freed me to do what I enjoy, to lay about the record books in 1981 without the accusation that I'm trying to justify myself in the only way I can. I want to go out this summer, not bothering about splits and pace-makers, and just do it myself as I did in 1979. The Olympics got in the way of that. They impose false restrictions. Throughout the winter of 1979–80 I was thinking of a span of six races in twelve days, rather than a one-off blinder. Of course, I finished up with a gold and a silver, and another world record, but it interrupted what I really enjoy doing. This time I hope not just to nibble the records but to improve them substantially. What I really want from athletics is an 800 metres in under 1:42, a 1,500 metres in under 3:30 and a mile in under 3:47. I did my bit last year in satisfying those who react primarily to the Olympics every four years, and unfairly rate an athlete's status exclusively by that performance. There have been some great athletes who never achieved anything in the Olympics. I want to run for myself, for the pure fun and exhil-

aration of running at speeds that have not been run
before. The Coe who crossed the line in Zürich in 1979
would have been fifty yards past the tape in Moscow.

Ironically, I think that running to win for so long, for
three years from 1977 to 1980, rather than running to
achieve fast times, has limited Steve: so that when he suddenly started to run with the specific intention of breaking
records he found it difficult. He does not have the same
ratio of records to attempts that I have – four records in
five attempts. Steve admitted in Koblenz that he couldn't
have done it without Wessinghage. It's my sincere hope
that I have yet to become a much improved runner. It is
records more than medals which excite me.

I don't have enough time to move up to the 5,000
metres in 1981. My intention is to get back the 1,500
metres and mile records and improve the 800 metres. If
everything goes right, this should be my best ever season,
after a winter of speed work and concentrating on *quality*.
I expect I will switch to the 5,000 metres after the 1982
European Championships. It is one of the great races of
the track. It's twelve and a half laps, and about thirteen
minutes is a nice time to be on the track, for the crowd to
get involved. With 1,500 metres the tactics are more
limited, the 5,000 metres offers greater flexibility. I don't
think anybody could run me out in the first mile, or the
last mile, so therefore the grey area is the three-and-a-half
laps in the middle. At present, a long run for home in the
5,000 metres is thought of as the last two laps. Why not
the last three?

Whether or not I run against Steve in 1981 depends on
a number of factors. It is obvious that a race between us,
over 1,500 metres or a mile, in a sponsored meeting, is
capable of generating a huge sum of money through television. It is my belief, however, that most of the revenue
ought to go back into athletics, rather than be syphoned
off by some PR consortium working in collaboration with
TV and advertising geared to programme ratings in
Britain or America. Advertising and TV both have their
part to play in giving athletics financial security, but I was
most disturbed by some of the things I heard about

arrangements for last year's Golden Mile at Crystal Palace, in which injury prevented me from running.

Television is also in a position to play a part in the development of athletics. There is an ever increasing likelihood that with such heavy emphasis on inter-channel rivalry, and the pursuit of viewing figures, commentaries will become unrealistic and uncritical. If something is on one channel, that channel's company wants it to be a 'good' race, in the way that boring goalless draws in soccer are sometimes built up by TV as fascinating tactical battles in a bid to hold viewers. But we should not lose sight of the fact that TV also offers a tremendous opportunity to give huge projection to the *right* image.❜

Late in 1979, Seb, as one of the dozen chief guests, attended the Man of the Year luncheon at the Savoy in London, a dignified charity function chaired by the Duke of Devonshire. Those being honoured beside the young runner who had broken three world records were men of letters, of valour, of research, of medicine. There was also disc jockey and radio presenter Jimmy Young. Seb sat back and listened to Frank Bough, the master of ceremonies, cite the accomplishments which had brought these men together: a famous physicist; a man who had reached the height of esteem in medicine in spite of being unable to read and write as a teenager because of dyslexia; a lifeboatman of unimaginable courage who was the first in history to win bronze, silver, and gold medals for gallantry; a policeman who had arrested armed raiders, been shot in the stomach and crawled to ring for help; a fireman who had held burning timbers while a colleague was rescued; an army captain who had lost both legs in Northern Ireland and was back on active service. Towards the end of the citation Seb and Jimmy Young caught each other's eyes, and Jimmy leaned over to say exactly what was also in Seb's mind: 'What on earth am I doing here?'

❝ I've never been so impressed with a group of people in my life. It was a lesson, it really did bring me back down to earth. It made me think how easy it is to become a household name, a well-known face, for doing very little in terms of general ability. We put a strange premium on fame in this country these days, it seems to me. People are famous merely for being well known, rather than for the true merit of what they have achieved. What I've done is not outstanding in anything other than the field in which I'm operating; and therefore I feel embarrassed about standing up in chat shows and such like and giving opinions on art, politics, or economics – subjects which I might feel I know a little bit about but not to the extent that I should impose my views on a vast audience. It's not false modesty, I just don't see the point unless somebody wants me specifically to discuss sport. I do what I do in athletics not just for the satisfaction of the world record or the gold medal, but to plumb the depths of myself and discover what my potential is as a person. But it surprises me that people are interested in a sportsman's views on unrelated subjects. I suppose that's the price of success!

Anybody should attempt to excel at whatever they do, but the measure of their success should not only be the public estimation of what they achieve, which has fixed stereotypes, but how close they come to their own potential. That is why, depending on your potential, it is possible to retire from athletics, say, with much less than an Olympic gold medal and be really satisfied. What was so crushing for me in Moscow when I lost the 800 metres was that I knew I had fallen so wretchedly short of my true ability.

I will retire after the World Championships in 1983 or the Olympics in 1984 because by then I will have spent enough time concentrating severely on one thing, and even then it might be too long. If I'd been twenty-six in Moscow instead of twenty-three I would have retired then. I realize that when I stop I run the risk of feeling unfulfilled, that I will miss the exhilaration of competition. One can get to a point where you need to feel extended almost to the point of breaking, but I will not want to linger on, being part of the 'fame industry'. Even if it becomes allowable for athletes to advertise I don't think I would want to sell my face; once I stop competing I want to be a private person. I admire Brendan for his refusal to fill his house with any discount goods he is offered, wanting the pride of knowing that he paid for the house, the car, and the furniture he has. It's just a kind of dignity, and I know there will be many people who say I am silly to feel this way.'

Seb accepts that athletes all have different levels of application as well as ability, and this is why he favours Open, rather than Professional, athletics.

'At the moment I also feel an element of responsibility in not getting out of athletics too soon. It's in a state of flux, I've never seen a sport so set up for destruction. We must not let it be handed over to the sharks, they're going to have to fight for it. I'm chairman of an off-shoot of the International Athletes Club whose aim is to try to help rationalize Open athletics when it comes, which it must.

I personally would never become a seven-day-a-week professional, because I would never wish to be under contract to anybody or be obliged to run. I would not want to sacrifice my freedom of action, my independence. But for a world-class athlete some of the rules and regulations on expenses are unnecessarily harsh in the costly world of today. Although I don't want a Packer-type circus, which would be crippling for the present framework of international athletics, I think there should be financial flexibility. I've never been able to see why, if you have a talent and you live in a free society, and there is a market for your talent, you should not be allowed to capitalize on it. However much sporting

academics and history buffs talk about the evils of
abolishing amateurism – and they are mostly over sixty! –
when you get down to it, you cannot *eat* goodwill, you
cannot get to the top in international sport today without
financial assistance, unless you have a rich father or wife!
I'm not even talking about Olympic medallists, but average
internationals needing nothing more than to break even. Of
course there are some internationals such as Dwight
Stones and Guy Drut who have admitted to making large
sums, even as amateurs. But solely professional athletics is
not on either; there must be a mixture of both, in open
sport, so that the pros, or those accepting money, are
always being challenged, and replaced, by those from
below in the normal way as in tennis, say.

The same athletes cannot compete over, say, 5,000
metres every few days, or with the frequency which
promoters would be looking for. If you see people running
too frequently, then it *must* be a con, because what is
happening out there on the track cannot be genuine.
There are lots of athletes around at the present moment
who are not running flat out at the big sponsored
international meetings, either because they are tired or
saving themselves. I have never yet run in a race where I
was not giving absolutely my best and attempting to win.
What is needed in open athletics is prize money rather
than appearance money, because prize money guarantees
a commitment. But the prize money should be graded
down to tenth place or so, because you need a field to
make a race and someone has to come last. A lot of the
sting would be taken out of the present problems if the
International Federation would relax the regulations on
advertising and endorsements, which is how sportsmen
like Borg and Ballesteros make so much of their money.
In that area, you certainly only get paid what you're
worth.

But there *must* be free interplay between the amateur
and the pro in athletics; under no circumstances should
those who want to run for fun, or who are not good
enough to command a fee, be frozen out. The youngsters
on the way up need the experience against the top

competitors in order to develop, just as I did when I was eighteen or nineteen, and was able to race against Walker, Quax, Dixon, and Bayi. Only in that way was I able to develop into an international athlete. It is bad to have a situation, as in professional snooker, where the pros control who gets a professional licence, because they don't want an unknown coming in and sweeping the table. Nor must we ever allow athletics to get like boxing, where managers and promoters control who gets to the top, who gets the fights. The only reason you should be able to run in an Olympic or World Championship 1,500 metres final is because you are good enough to be there. But in the present sham-amateur world it's difficult to get to the top without getting caught up in the twilight area of ducking and diving; it obliges honest people to become dishonest. I've been fortunate initially to have tremendous support from my parents, and latterly sponsorship from the Sports Aid Foundation and Otis, who helped to make possible my preparation for the Olympics.

The importance of my gold medal in Moscow was not just my own pride, but the position of influence I hope it gives me to help shape athletics, to prevent it becoming a promoter's and sponsor's carve-up, to keep it open for young people coming up so that they can get races without being told when, where and even *how* they must run. If you become famous it gives you an obligation. You don't ask to be famous (though perhaps some do), but if you are then you should accept the burden which goes with it, as Mary Peters has done in Belfast. The power to influence is enormous and it has to be used the right way. We do not want a generation of young athletes who think it is smart to come waving down the finishing straight as we saw in last year's English Schools championships. I don't feel like leaving the sport and turning it over to some of the people who are in it at the moment. There is a misguided battle going on between officials wanting to preserve old fashioned amateurism on the one hand, which can only ultimately hasten the commercial take-over, and those who are not in the race to win but to see who can make the first million, on the other hand.

It is inevitable that athletics *will* go Open, but it is vital
that it does not just become a licence to print money for
the leading competitors and a handful of promoters and
advertising agents collaborating with television. All of us
at the top, including Ovett, Thompson, and Wells, ought
to be thinking very carefully not only of ourselves, but of
what sort of sport we want to hand on to the next
generation. It is vital that the young runners of enormous
potential which Britain possesses just below the highest
level, such as Dave Warren, Steve Cram, Graham Williamson, and Gary Oakes, and all those coming through
behind them, should be free to develop in the races and
over the distances they need, without being required to
accommodate the demands of promotors and sponsors. Of
course sponsors have to receive value for money, but sport
has to remain sport, a concept rooted on the track and not
in the balance sheet. It must not become another
consumer-entertainment package. In all sports we have to
protect the fundamentals of sportsmanship, self-
determination of the individual and the pursuit of excellence free of commercial expediency, and as Voltaire said,
'the price of freedom is eternal vigilance'.

On 11 February, 1981, running for Great Britain against
East Germany in an indoor meeting at RAF Cosford, Seb
set a new 800 metres indoor world record of 1:46·0,
improving the four-year-old record of Carlo Grippo of Italy
by 0·5. It was a superlative, flowing run against former
Moscow rivals Andreas Busse and Detlef Wagenknecht,
proving that his back injury was totally recovered and that
he was on course for an exciting summer.

APPENDIX A

A complete list of the track races in which Sebastian Coe
has competed since 1973, when he was sixteen

Abbreviations

pb–personal best	sf–semi final	UK–United Kingdom record
h–heat	cr–championship record	WR–World record
f–final	CR–Commonwealth record	

Date	Event	Track	Distance	Place	Time
1973					
17 March	UK Indoor Championships	Cosford	800 m	4th	2:25.0
1 May	B..Milers' Club	Stretford	800 m	3rd	1:56.6
5 May	Longwood Youth	Huddersfield	1,500 m	1st	4:7.4
13 May	B. Milers' Club	Crystal Palace	800 m	2nd	1:56.0 (pb)
18 May	West District Schools	Sheffield	800 m	1st	2:1.1
18 May	West District Schools	Sheffield	1,500 m	1st	4:15.4
23 May	Sheffield Selection	Sheffield	3,000 m	1st	8:43.7
3 June	Northern League	Sheffield	1,500 m	3rd	4:7.5
9 June	Yorks Schools Championships	York	3,000 m	1st	8:49.0
16 June	N. Counties	Sheffield	1,500 m	3rd	3:59.5 (pb)
7 July	English Schools	Bebington	3,000 m	1st	8:40.2 (pb)
17 July	S. Yorks League	Doncaster	800 m	1st	1:59.7
21 July	City Championships	Sheffield	800 m	1st	1:57.0
21 July	City Championships	Sheffield	1,500 m	1st	4:7.4
4 Aug	AAA Youth Championships	Aldersley	1,500 m	1st	3:55.0 (pb)
14 Aug	Stretford League	Manchester	3,000 m	6th	8:34.6 (pb)
9 Sept	Hallam Harriers Ch'ships	Sheffield	400 m		51.8 (pb)
15 Sept	Rotherham Festival	Rotherham	1,500 m	1st	3:58.0
1974					
10 April	Training run	Rotherham	800 m		1:55.1 (pb)
April–Nov Injured with stress fractures					
1975					
21 March	Indoor Under 20 Ch'ships	Cosford	1,500 m (h)	2nd	4:8.0
22 March	Indoor Under 20 Ch'ships	Cosford	1,500 m (f)	1st	3:54.4 (pb)
13 April	Pye Cup	Cleckheaton	1,500 m	1st	3:49.7 (pb)

Date	Event	Track	Distance	Place	Time
30 April	B. Milers' Club	Rawtenstall	1,500 m	1st	3:54.0
31 May	Yorks Senior Championships	Cleckheaton	1,500 m	1st	3:51.3
8 June	Pye Cup	Cleckheaton	800 m	1st	1:53.8 (pb)
8 June	Pye Cup	Cleckheaton	4 × 400 m		50.5
21 June	N. Counties Under 20	Gateshead	1,500 m	1st	3:50.8
25 June	Northern League	Sheffield	300 m	2nd	36.2 (pb)
28 June	N. Counties Under 20	Blackburn	3,000 m	1st	8:14.2 (pb)
26 July	AAA Junior Championships	Kirkby	1,500 m (h)	1st	3:52.0
27 July	AAA Junior Championships	Kirkby	1,500 m (f)	1st	3:49.1 (pb)
30 July	GB v France/Spain	Warley	1,500 m	1st	3:50.3
23 Aug	European Junior Ch'ships	Athens	1,500 m (h)		3:48.0 (pb)
24 Aug	European Junior Ch'ships	Athens	1,500 m (f)	3rd	3:45.2 (pb)

1976

Date	Event	Track	Distance	Place	Time
24 Jan	UK Indoor Championships	Cosford	1,500 m	5th	3:51.0
6 March	Loughborough Match	Crystal Palace	4 × 800 m		1:52.0 (pb)
20 March	Loughborough Match	Cosford	600 relay/leg		80.4 (pb)
28 March	B. Milers' Club	Stretford	1,500 m	1st	3:47.4
14 April	H. Wilson Mile	Crystal Palace	1 mile	1st	4:7.6
1 May	B. Milers' Club	Stretford	1 mile	1st	4:5.7
12 May	Loughborough Match	Loughborough	800 m	1st	1:53.0
16 May	Yorkshire Championships	Cleckheaton	1,500 m	1st	3:43.3 (pb)
19 May	Loughborough v Borough Rd	Isleworth	800 m	1st	1:53.0
31 May	Inter-Counties Championships	Crystal Palace	1 mile	2nd	4:2.4 (pb)
11 June	Olympic Selection	Crystal Palace	1,500 m	7th	3:43.2 (pb)
17 June	Loughborough v AAA	Loughborough	800 m	1st	1:50.7 (pb)
24 July	Heckington Sports	Heckington	1 mile	1st	4:9.1
1 Aug	Open Meeting	Nottingham	1,000 m	1st	2:30.0
8 Aug	B. Milers' Club	Stretford	800 m	1st	1:47.7 (pb)
13 Aug	AAA Championships	Crystal Palace	1,500 m (h)	3rd	3:45.05
14 Aug	AAA Championships	Crystal Palace	1,500 m (f)	4th	3:42.6 (pb)
21 Aug	Rediffusion Games	Gateshead	1 mile	3rd	4:1.7 (pb)
30 Aug	Emsley Carr Mile	Crystal Palace	1 mile	7th	3:58.3 (pb)
14 Sept	Bell's Games	Gateshead	1 mile	2nd	4:0.5

1977

Date	Event	Track	Distance	Place	Time
29 Jan	UK Indoor Championships	Cosford	800 m	1st	1:49.1 (pb/cr)
19 Feb	GB v W. Germany	Dortmund	800 m	1st	1:47.6 (CR)

Date	Event	Track	Distance	Place	Time
26 Feb	GB v France	Cosford	800 m	1st	1:47.5 (CR)
12 March	European Indoor Ch'ships	San Sebastian	800 m (h)	1st	1:50.5
13 March	European Indoor Ch'ships	San Sebastian	800 m (sf)	1st	1:48.25
14 March	European Indoor Ch'ships	San Sebastian	800 m (f)	1st	1:46.54 (CR)
3 July	Dewhurst Games	Spalding	800 m	1st	1:51.7
23 July	AAA Championships	Crystal Palace	800 m	2nd	1:46.8
30 July	Philips Games	Gateshead	800 m	2nd	1:47.4
14 Aug	Europa Cup	Helsinki	800 m	4th	1:47.6
16 Aug	Ivo Van Damme	Brussels	800 m	3rd	1:46.3 (pb)
24 Aug	Club Meeting	Rotherham	400 m	1st	49.1
28 Aug	GB v W. Germany	Crystal Palace	800 m	1st	1:47.8
29 Aug	Emsley Carr Mile	Crystal Palace	1 mile	1st	3:57.7 (pb)
7 Sept	Courage Games	St Ives	800 m	1st	1:48.1
9 Sept	Coca-Cola	Crystal Palace	800 m	2nd	1:44.95 (UK)

1978

Date	Event	Track	Distance	Place	Time
26 April	Loughborough Match	Loughborough	400 m	1st	48.0 (pb)
10 May	Loughborough Match	Isleworth	400 m	1st	47.7 (pb)
14 May	Yorkshire Championships	Cleckheaton	800 m	1st	1:45.6 (CR)
1 June	Loughborough v AAA	Loughborough	800 m	1st	1:50.0
9 July	Philips Games	Gateshead	800 m	1st	1:46.8
15 July	UK Championships	Meadowbank	800 m	1st	1:47.1
9 Aug	International Invitation	Viareggio	800 m	1st	1:45.7
18 Aug	Ivo Van Damme	Brussels	800 m	1st	1:44.26 (UK)
31 Aug	European Championships	Prague	800 m	3rd	1:44.8
15 Sept	Coca-Cola	Crystal Palace	800 m	1st	1:43.97 (UK)
17 Sept	McEwans Games	Gateshead	1 mile	1st	4:2.2

1979

Date	Event	Track	Distance	Place	Time
27 Jan	UK Indoor Championships	Cosford	3,000 m	1st	7:59.8
25 April	Loughborough Match	Crystal Palace	400 m	2nd	48.3
20 May	Yorkshire Championships	Cleckheaton	800 m	1st	1:50.5
21 May	Yorkshire Championships	Cleckheaton	400 m	1st	47.6 (pb)
23 May	Loughborough Match	Loughborough	400 m	1st	47.4 (pb)
23 May	Loughborough Match	Loughborough	800 m	1st	1:54.8
31 May	Loughborough v AAA	Loughborough	800 m	1st	1:47.8
16 June	N. Counties Championships	Costeloe Park	800 m	1st	1:46.3
30 June	Europa Cup	Malmo	800 m (sf)	1st	1:46.63

Date	Event	Track	Distance	Place	Time
3 July	Bislet Games	Oslo	800 m	1st	1:42.33 (WR)
14 July	AAA Championships	Crystal Palace	400 m	2nd	46.85 (pb)
17 July	Golden Mile	Oslo	1 mile	1st	3:48.95 (WR)
5 Aug	International Invitation	Viareggio	800 m	1st	1:50.0
8 Aug	Europa Cup	Turin	800 m (f)	1st	1:47.3
15 Aug	Weltklasse	Zürich	1,500 m	1st	3:32.03 (WR)

1980

Date	Event	Track	Distance	Place	Time
26 April	Loughborough Match	Crystal Palace	3,000 m	1st	7:57.4
7 May	Loughborough Match	Isleworth	1,500 m	1st	3:45.1
11 May	Yorkshire Championships	Cudworth	5,000 m	1st	14:6.0
21 May	England v Belgium	Crystal Palace	800 m	1st	1:47.5
25 May	Inter-Counties Championships	Birmingham	800 m (h)	1st	1:49.0
26 May	Inter-Counties Championships	Birmingham	800 m (f)	1st	1:45.41
1 June	International Invitation	Turin	800 m	1st	1:45.8
5 June	Loughborough v AAA	Loughborough	800 m	1st	1:44.98
7 June	N. Counties	Cleckheaton	800 m	1st	1:44.7
14 June	UK Championships	Crystal Palace	400 m	2nd	47.0
1 July	Bislet Games	Oslo	1,000 m	1st	2:13.4 (WR)
24 July	Olympic Games	Moscow	800 m (h)	1st	1:48.5
25 July	Olympic Games	Moscow	800 m (sf)	2nd	1:46.7
26 July	Olympic Games	Moscow	800 m (f)	2nd	1:45.9
30 July	Olympic Games	Moscow	1,500 m (h)	2nd	3:40.1
31 July	Olympic Games	Moscow	1,500 m (sf)	1st	3:39.4
1 Aug	Olympic Games	Moscow	1,500 m (f)	1st	3:38.4
8 Aug	Coca-Cola	Crystal Palace	800 m	1st	1:45.0
13 Aug	Weltklasse	Zürich	1,500 m	1st	3:32.19
14 Aug	International Invitation	Viareggio	800 m	2nd	1:45.01

1981

Date	Event	Track	Distance	Place	Time
24 Jan	AAA Indoor Championships	Cosford	3,000 m	1st	7:55.2
11 Feb	GB v GDR (Indoor)	Cosford	800 m	1st	1:46.0 (WR)

APPENDIX B
Evolution of World Records
800 metres

Time	Runner	Nation	Date	Place
1:51.9	Ted Meredith	USA	8.7.1912	Stockholm
1:51.6	Otto Peltzer	Germany	3.7.1926	London
1:50.6	Séra Martin	France	14.7.1928	Paris
1:49.8	Tom Hampson	GB	2.8.1932	Los Angeles
1:49.8	Ben Eastman	USA	16.6.1934	Princeton
1:49.7	Glenn Cunningham	USA	20.8.1936	Stockholm
1:49.6	Elroy Robinson	USA	11.7.1937	New York
1:48.4	Sydney Wooderson	GB	20.8.1938	Motspur Park
1:46.6	Rudolf Harbig	Germany	15.7.1939	Milan
1:45.7	Roger Moens	Belgium	3.8.1955	Oslo
1:44.3	Peter Snell	New Zealand	3.2.1962	Christchurch
1:44.3	Ralph Doubell	Australia	15.10.1968	Mexico City
1:44.3	Dave Wottle	USA	1.7.1972	Eugene
1:43.7	Marcello Fiasconaro	Italy	27.6.1973	Milan
1:43.5	Alberto Juantorena	Cuba	25.7.1976	Montreal
1:43.44	Alberto Juantorena	Cuba	21.8.1977	Sofia
1:42.33	Sebastian Coe	GB	3.7.1979	Oslo

1,000 metres

Time	Runner	Nation	Date	Place
2:32.3	Georg Mickler	Germany	22.6.1913	Hanover
2:29.1	Anatole Bolin	Sweden	22.9.1918	Stockholm
2:28.6	Sven Lundgren	Sweden	27.9.1922	Stockholm
2:26.8	Séra Martin	France	30.9.1926	Paris
2:25.8	Otto Peltzer	Germany	18.9.1927	Paris
2:23.6	Jules Ladoumègue	France	19.10.1930	Paris
2:21.5	Rudolf Harbig	Germany	24.5.1941	Dresden
2:21.4	Rune Gustafsson	Sweden	4.9.1946	Borås
2:21.4	Marcel Hansenne	France	27.8.1948	Gothenburg
2:21.3	Olle Åberg	Sweden	10.8.1952	Copenhagen
2:21.2	Stanislav Jungwirth	Czechoslovakia	27.10.1952	Stará Boleslav
2:20.8	Mal Whitfield	USA	16.8.1953	Eskilstuna

Time	Runner	Nation	Date	Place
2:20.4	Audun Boysen	Norway	17.9.1953	Oslo
2:19.5	Audun Boysen	Norway	18.8.1954	Gävle
2:19.0	Audun Boysen	Norway	30.8.1955	Gothenburg
2:19.0	István Rózsavölgyi	Hungary	21.9.1955	Tata
2:18.1	Dan Waern	Sweden	19.9.1958	Turku
2:17.8	Dan Waern	Sweden	21.8.1959	Karlstad
2:16.7	Siegfried Valentin	GDR	19.7.1960	Potsdam
2:16.6	Peter Snell	New Zealand	12.11.1964	Auckland
2:16.2	Jürgen May	GDR	20.7.1965	Erfurt
2:16.2	Franz-Josef Kemper	Germany	21.9.1966	Hanover
2:16.0	Daniel Malan	South Africa	24.6.1973	Munich
2:13.9	Rick Wohlhuter	USA	30.7.1974	Oslo
2:13.4	Sebastian Coe	GB	1.7.1980	Oslo

1,500 metres

Time	Runner	Nation	Date	Place
3:55.8	Abel Kiviat	USA	8.6.1912	Cambridge, Mass
3:54.7	John Zander	Sweden	5.8.1917	Stockholm
3:52.6	Paavo Nurmi	Finland	19.6.1924	Helsinki
3:51.0	Otto Peltzer	Germany	11.9.1926	Berlin
3:49.2	Jules Ladoumègue	France	5.10.1930	Paris
3:49.2	Luigi Beccali	Italy	9.9.1933	Turin
3:49.0	Luigi Beccali	Italy	17.9.1933	Milan
3:48.8	Bill Bonthron	USA	30.6.1934	Milwaukee
3:47.8	Jack Lovelock	New Zealand	6.8.1936	Berlin
3:47.6	Gunder Hägg	Sweden	10.8.1941	Stockholm
3:45.8	Gunder Hägg	Sweden	17.7.1942	Stockholm
3:45.0	Arne Andersson	Sweden	17.8.1943	Gothenburg
3:43.0	Gunder Hägg	Sweden	7.7.1944	Gothenburg
3:43.0	Lennart Strand	Sweden	15.7.1947	Malmö
3:43.0	Werner Lueg	Germany	29.6.1952	Berlin
3:42.8	Wes Santee	USA	4.6.1954	Compton
3:41.8	John Landy	Australia	21.6.1954	Turku
3:40.8	Sándor Iharos	Hungary	28.7.1955	Helsinki
3:40.8	Lásló Tábori	Hungary	6.9.1955	Oslo

APPENDIX B 169

Time	Runner	Nation	Date	Place
3:40.8	Gunnar Nielson	Denmark	6.9.1955	Oslo
3:40.6	István Rózsavölgyi	Hungary	3.8.1956	Tata
3:40.2	Olavi Salsola	Finland	11.7.1957	Turku
3:40.2	Olavi Salonen	Finland	11.7.1957	Turku
3:38.1	Stanislav Jungwirth	Czechoslovakia	12.7.1957	Stará Boleslav
3:36.0	Herb Elliott	Australia	28.8.1958	Gothenburg
3:35.6	Herb Elliott	Australia	6.9.1960	Rome
3:33.1	Jim Ryun	USA	8.7.1967	Los Angeles
3:32.2	Filbert Bayi	Tanzania	2.2.1974	Christchurch
3:32.1	Sebastian Coe	GB	15.8.1979	Oslo
3:31.4	Steve Ovett	GB	27.8.1980	Koblenz

1 mile

Time	Runner	Nation	Date	Place
4:14.4	John Paul Jones	USA	31.5.1913	Cambridge, Mass
4:12.6	Norman Taber	USA	16.7.1915	Cambridge, Mass
4:10.4	Paavo Nurmi	Finland	23.8.1923	Stockholm
4:09.2	Jules Ladoumègue	France	4.10.1931	Paris
4:07.6	Jack Lovelock	New Zealand	15.7.1933	Princeton
4:06.8	Glenn Cunningham	USA	16.6.1934	Princeton
4:06.4	Sydney Wooderson	GB	28.8.1937	Motspur Park
4:06.2	Gunder Hägg	Sweden	1.7.1942	Gothenburg
4:06.2	Arne Andersson	Sweden	10.7.1942	Stockholm
4:04.6	Gunder Hägg	Sweden	4.9.1942	Stockholm
4:02.6	Arne Andersson	Sweden	1.7.1943	Gothenburg
4:01.6	Arne Andersson	Sweden	18.7.1944	Malmö
4:01.4	Gunder Hägg	Sweden	17.7.1945	Malmö
3:59.4	Roger Bannister	GB	6.5.1954	Oxford
3:58.0	John Landy	Australia	21.6.1954	Turku
3:57.2	Derek Ibbotson	GB	19.7.1957	London
3:54.5	Herb Elliott	Australia	6.8.1958	Dublin
3:54.4	Peter Snell	New Zealand	27.1.1962	Wanganui
3:54.1	Peter Snell	New Zealand	17.11.1964	Auckland
3:53.6	Michel Jazy	France	9.6.1965	Rennes
3:51.3	Jim Ryun	USA	17.7.1966	Berkeley

Time	Runner	Nation	Date	Place
3:51.1	Jim Ryun	USA	23.6.1967	Bakersfield
3:51.0	Filbert Bayi	Tanzania	17.5.1975	Kingston
3:49.4	John Walker	New Zealand	12.8.1975	Gothenburg
3:49.0	Sebastian Coe	GB	17.7.1979	Oslo
3:48.8	Steve Ovett	GB	1.7.1980	Oslo

Index

Coleman, David, 112, 129
Cooper, Henry, 16, 118
Cooper, Peter, 75
Coubertin, Baron de, 102
Cousins, Robin, 60
Cram, Steve, 50, 97, 130, 131–2,
   139, 140, 141, 162
Cunningham, Glenn, 79

Daily Express, 13, 16, 94, 124,
   133
Daily Mail, 116, 144
Daily Mirror, 50, 75
Daily Telegraph, 31, 49, 94, 111
Davies, Dickie, 145
Davies, Lynn, 64, 107, 136
Davies, Sharon, 12
Dixon, Rod, 47, 65–6, 69, 74,
   161
Drut, Guy, 160
Durham, Bishop of, 145

Elliott, Herb, 33, 43
Enyeart, Mark, 50
Evening Standard, 73

Farrell, Mike, 50
Fiasconaro, Marcello, 54
Flynn, Raymond, 154
Follows, Sir Denis, 93–4
Fontanella, Vittorio, 130–2,
   140–1
Foster, Brendan, 13, 20, 55, 56,
   57, 60, 64, 66, 74, 76, 82, 104,
   129, 137, 152, 159
Fox, Norman, 144
Francis, Gerry, 97
Franklin, Eddie, 97

Gandy, George, 30, 34–5, 47,
   50–1, 63, 80, 84, 92, 137
Gerschler, 42
Gilkés, James, 78
Gonzales, Alexandre, 68
Goodhew, Duncan, 12
Goodman, Douglas, 64
Grippo, Carlo, 48, 162
Guardian, The, 58, 97, 123
Guimaraes, Alberto, 110, 114

Hägg, Gunder, 46, 79
Hague, Ian, 29, 97
Hague, Robert, 30
Harbig, Rudolph, 64
Hart, Colin, 119
Hartman, Marea, 48
Hassan, Kashif, 68
Haukvik, Arne, 64, 69
Heffernan, Danny, 27–8
Hemery, David, 25
Henson, John, 30
Hermens, Jos, 62
Hewson, Brian, 50
Higgins, Laurie, 84–5
Hildreth, Peter, 123, 144
Hill, Benny, 127
Hooper, Brian, 63
Hubbard, Alan, 94
Humphreys, Professor John, 91

Ibbotson, Derek, 13, 33
International Athletes Club, 80,
   146, 159
Ishii, Takashi, 70

James, Clive, 117
Jelley, Arch, 101
Jenkins, David, 46, 54, 58
Johnson, Derek, 146
Joseph, Dane, 57
Juantorena, Alberto, 52, 53, 59,
   66

Keegan, Kevin, 85
Keino, Kip, 46, 144
Killanin, Lord, 102, 123
Kirov, Nikolai, 108–10, 114–16
Koskei, Kip, 78–9
Kuts, Vladimir, 46

Lacy, Steve, 69–71, 101
Landy, John, 46
Lawton, James, 120
Loikanen, Antii, 130
Lovelock, Jack, 146
Lydiard, Arthur, 35

McDonald, Linsey, 136, 153

Tischenko, Vitaly, 131
Track and Field News, 74

Uttley, Roger, 97

Van Damme, Ivo, 50, 52
Vasala, Pekka, 144
Viren, Lasse, 128

Wagenknecht, Detlef, 108–10,
 114–16, 124, 162
Waitz, Grete, 65
Waitz, Jack, 65
Walker, John, 14, 46, 49, 57, 65,
 68–9, 70, 71–4, 100–1, 117,
 133, 145, 154, 161
Walker, Mrs, 99
Warren, Dave, 97–8, 99–100,
 108–10, 113, 115, 162
Watman, Mel, 45, 118, 124
Wells, Allan, 12, 75, 78, 136, 152,
 162

Wells, Margot, 12
Wessinghage, Tom, 57, 61, 69,
 71, 101, 155–6
White, Evans, 65
Whitehead, Nick, 107, 136
Whitfield, Mal, 14
Wilkinson, Walter, 31
Williamson, Graham, 50, 68–71,
 73, 80, 99–100, 162
Wilson, Harry, 53, 57, 111, 131
Wohlhuter, Rick, 67, 98
Wooderson, Sydney, 32, 79
Wooldridge, Ian, 116, 144
Wulbeck, Willi, 49, 56, 75–6,
 98–9

Yakoylev, Pavel, 130
Yifter, Miruts, 128
Young, Jimmy, 157

Zivotic, D., 76
Zdravkovic, Dragan, 130, 132,
 139, 140